Our Children's Keepers

By the same author:

Street Kids, by Larry Cole,
with Ralph, Pauli,
Eddie, & Charlie

Larry Cole

Our Children's Keepers

Inside America's Kid Prisons

Grossman Publishers
New York
1972

ACKNOWLEDGMENT
Simon & Schuster, Inc.: From *Pogo Stepmother Goose* by Walt Kelly.
Copyright © 1954 by Walt Kelly. Reprinted by permission of Simon and
Schuster.

To Mom and Dad,
who taught me that there will only be justice
when those who are not injured are as indignant
as those who are

Acknowledgments

Several people helped get this book started. Deborah Greenberg, whose love for kids and belief in my ability to speak for them gave me the first push, helped me to obtain the support of the Norman Foundation, which supported much of my travel and research.

Off and on my way, I met many people who helped me uncover the facts about kids and their prisons, many of whom gave me information while putting themselves in economic or physical danger. Others spent the time to introduce me to kids, to people working with them, and to people who knew where I should look. For obvious reasons I will not name them here, but since each of them will see this book, I want them to know how much their unselfish and sometimes risky support of this work meant to its formulation and conclusion. Among several unexpected, hopeful discoveries I made in my travels through the world of kid prisons, one of the most important was the good people hiding within the system. Maybe someday soon you'll be able to come out.

Thanks to George Cronin, Lolas Elie, Gilbert Ballejos, Norman Linton, and Jim Crawford for getting me people and information that I could never have found alone. Thanks also to the American Public Health Association and Robert H. Bremner for publishing and editing the best history of children's institutions ever put together, the three-volume *Children and Youth in America: A Documentary History*.

And of course, thanks to the kids who, both in and out of the jails they told me about, risked most of all. Happily, all my inside sources are now out. I hope they stay out. I hope the kids on the outside who spoke with me about their past experiences will keep them in the past. Their willing energies always gave me renewed hope when the collective effect of those depressing institutions was making me feel uncharacteristically hopeless.

To Stu Black, my closest friend and fighter for kids, whose dedication has never been compromised even when pressures put on him would have stopped other men.

To Michelle, whose notion of commitment to an idea is to live it every day, and who has taught me since I've lived with her, the dangers and the powers of tenacity.

And to the people at LEAP, Jill Marshall, Gus Seelig, Dakar Washington, and others of our affinity family, who helped in the daily details that determine whether advocacy of any kind will succeed after all the heroics and rhetoric are forgotten.

Contents

xi

Perspectives

The institutions that imprison children in America are both the result and the cause of more complex and socially disastrous problems. At worst, the institutions are processing children to their deaths. At best, they are warehousing them like tiny time bombs, shipping them out from time to time to explode, with unpredictable injuries. That is all any research can tell you about children's prisons—those hundreds of institutions that lock up children and call themselves training schools, detention centers, youth study or guidance centers, or reformatories.

In every city and state you can read about these jails for children. Banner headlines tell you of deaths, beatings, rapes, drugs, and riots. Even a public that has become calloused to violence on the 6 o'clock news still sits up and notices when children, many no more than infants, are involved. The public response to this recurring nausea has been to take a dose of research and commission study, hoping that this prescription will cure the sickness.

If there is one thing a person coughing to death of polluted air doesn't need, it's a study to determine whether the air is polluted. A black man in New York City doesn't need a study to tell him that there is discrimination in the North. A young Puerto Rican laughs when he's told that people are studying his ghetto school to see if they're teaching him right. Research, for people affected by an immediate problem, is an abstraction that has little redeeming value. In our nation, bogged down in a mire of seemingly insoluble problems, research has become a way to give lip service to a quest for solutions without having to give up anything or change anything. It's true that some research documents do end with recommendations, but these are generally so vague and nondirective that no one is made really uncomfortable. For whatever deep and mysterious political reasons, reports on institutions always seem to protect the guilty while condemning the innocent to at least another round of research.

Studies have turned out to be rationalizations for immobility rather than work preliminary to and necessary for action. Most of all, they've come to stand for personal blamelessness. The recurring enemy is "the system." But for the one hundred thousand children locked in prisons, it is not the system that keeps them awake or crying. It is not the system that beats them or locks them up for "crimes" no more serious than truancy. The system is a way to make things less personal and more comfortable for the people watching the horror stories on the late news.

Many systems, including the one that imprisons children, need to be changed. Many of them need to be totally eliminated. But people make systems work or not work. This book is about those people. What started out to be a survey of some thirty kid jails throughout the United States has become a set of portraits and profiles of people I met and found out about in a few of them. It was clear after the first three or four schools that there was an unexpected pattern: what began as an indictment of a system became instead a description of the people who make it what it is and what it will be. What began as a bitter resignation to a long and terrible battle to change conditions under which imprisoned children are forced to live became a much more hopeful search for people who could make change happen.

There are better statistical sources and compilations around than this book. They will tell you how much and how many and from where and how old and what color and generally how much is being done for so little. Whatever facts you're looking for, there is some kind of publication around now in which to find them.

What you will find here, instead, is a view of those we have chosen as keepers for our children and something of the kids' view of the places where they are kept.

If we take the Connecticut Blue Laws of 1650 as a starting point, we can view the development of treatment facilities for "delinquent youth" in America and may get some idea of the tradition subsequent innovations have been built on. The Code of 1650 was explicit about the punishment of "stubborne and rebellious" children:

> If any man have a stubborne and rebellious sonne of sufficient years and understanding which will not obey the voice of his father or the voice of his mother, and that when they have chastened him will not harken unto them, then may his father and mother lay hold on him and bring him to the Magistrates assembled in Courte, and testifie unto them that theire sonne is stubborne and rebellious and will not obey theire voice and Chastisement, but lives in sundry notorious Crimes, such a sonne shall bee put to death.
>
> It is also ordered by this courte and authority therof, that whatsoever Childe or servant within these Libberties, shall be convicted of any stubborne or rebellious carriage against their parents or governors, which is a forrunner of the aformentioned evills, the Governor or any two Magistrates have libberty and power from this Courte to commit such person or persons to the House of Correction and there to remaine under hard labour and severe punishment so long as the Courte or the major parte of the Magistrates shall judge meete.

While the specific means employed by the courts as agents for families and communities have changed a bit, the intent and severity have not.

Through the colonial period, the American revolution, and the first years of the republic, children were housed in the same facilities and cells as adult criminals. In some, liquor was sold to those who could afford it, and inmates were released only when they had paid for their keep. There were those who criticized the set-up, who worried about the bad effects of locking up kids, whose crimes were against authority, with robbers and violent criminals. But the talk, for more than a century, brought no reforms.

In 1823 James W. Gerard, a young attorney, and Isaac Collins, a Quaker and member of the Society for the Prevention of Pauperism, moved to establish the first institution for juvenile delinquents in the United States. Realizing that the "Bridewell"—the nineteenth-century equivalent of today's county jails—served only to increase a child's knowledge of and capacity for crime, Gerard and Collins recommended that a "house of refuge" be established. In 1824 such an institution was created by the legislature in New York, but it took more than five years before any substantial public support would be made available. In the interim the Society for the Prevention of Pauperism, by then the Society for the Reformation of Juvenile Delinquents in the City of New York, took up collections throughout the city.

While the House of Refuge gave children a separate place in which to be punished, it did not offer separate kinds of punishments. In his book, *Children in Urban Society*, Joseph M. Hawes spells out some of them:

> Methods of discipline varied; the Superintendent sometimes put the "subjects" on a ball and chain. He also used handcuffs, leg irons, and "the barrel." On January 28,

1825, Superintendent Curtis noted in his daily journal that six subjects, two of whom were girls, had been talking during a meal. He "took each of them to the barrel which supports them while the feet are tied on one side and the hands on the other . . . with the pantaloons down. . . . [This device] gives a convenient surface for the operation of the six-line cat. . . ."

Curtis also gave one "sullen, ill-natured and disobedient" girl "a dose of salts," apparently aloes, a purgative. She did not "transgress in things of importance" but she was "artful and sly" and told many "equivocating stories." Her conduct exasperated Superintendent Curtis and he "gave her a ball and chain and confined her to the house."

The first House of Refuge was not a secure place and, to keep some semblance of security, the superintendent appointed some of the boys to be guards. In a few years, more money would be allocated to provide for a new, more secure, facility. From that point, a time line from that first institution for juvenile delinquents to the present institutions would show more similarities than differences in the daily lives of the kids placed in them. You will come across cruel punishments again, and institutional requests for buildings that are more secure. You will meet children used as guards, and forced into programs sold to the public as "rehabilitative" that were never more than compulsive and joyless covers for punishment.

In 1835, in its Tenth Annual Report, the New York Society for the Reformation of Juvenile Delinquents described a routine day in the House of Refuge. You may find a striking resemblance, as I did, between this routine day and the routine day for girls in Mount View School in Denver, or for the kids at Scotlandville or Youth House. One hundred and thirty-five years have provided little change.

At sunrise the children are warned, by the ringing of a bell, to rise from their beds. Each child makes his own bed and steps forth, on a signal, into the Hall. They then proceed, in perfect order, to the Wash Room. Thence they are marched to parade in the Yard and undergo an examination as to their dress and cleanliness; after which they attend morning prayer. The morning school then commences where they are occupied in summer until 7 o'clock. A short intermission is allowed, when the bell rings for breakfast; after which they proceed to their respective workshops where they labour until twelve o'clock when they are called from work and one hour is allowed them for washing and eating their dinner. At one, they again commence work and continue at it until five in the afternoon when the labours of the day terminate. Half an hour is allowed for washing and eating their supper, and at half past five they are conducted to the school room where they continue at their studies until 8 o'clock. Evening prayer is performed by the Superintendant after which the children are conducted to their dormitories which they enter and are locked up for the night when perfect silence reigns throughout the establishment. The foregoing is the history of a single day and will answer for every day in the year except Sundays with slight variations during stormy weather and the short days in Winter.

The Refuge movement spread north to Boston and south to Baltimore and became the public-private merger solution to the growing number of homeless and troublesome street kids. As it spread, cruel and archaic practices spread with it. What started as a good idea based on real and pressing needs became, in the hands of people interested more in their jobs and an image of order, very much like what it was designed to replace.

From time to time, certain people risked their jobs and more to bring to light the problems of these children's prisons. One such man was the assistant superintendent of the New York House of Refuge, Elijah Devoe, who wrote in 1848 on conditions in his institution. He discussed the practice of locking kids away for indeterminate sentences, a practice that remains the norm today.

> In a conversation with a boy who made one of the most desperate attempts to escape that occurred while I was at the institution, he told me that if he knew how long he had to remain, he could reconcile himself to his punishment; but that he could not endure to have his mind constantly racked by uncertainty and suspense. He would rather by far be in State Prison, he said, for then he would know how long he should have to remain.

Devoe went on to give his views on the effect of the Refuge on its children. He commented on the usual rationalization that "those" kids knew no better and, in fact, were contented with conditions there.

> Are children happy in the Refuge? There is scarcely any conceivable position in life that would render a human being entirely and uninterruptedly wretched. Complete misery destroys; elasticity of human nature is so great that any state which is endurable, becomes daily more tolerable, until at length it affords intervals of pleasure. Although to children, life in the refuge is dark and stormy, still, in general they know how to avail themselves of all facilities that afford present enjoyment; and do not fail to bask in those rays of sunshine which occasionally light up and warm their dreary path. But nothing short of excessive ignorance can entertain for a moment the idea that the inmates of the Refuge are contented. In summer, they are about fourteen hours under orders daily. On parade, at table, at their work, and in school, they are not allowed to converse. They rise at five o'clock in the summer, are hurried into the yard—hurried into the dining room— hurried at their work and at their studies. For every trifling commission or omission which it is deemed wrong to do or to omit to do, they are "cut" with ratan. Every day they experience a series of painful excitements. The

endurance of the whip or the loss of a meal—deprivation
of play or the solitary cell. On every hand their walk is
bounded; while Restriction and Constraint are their most
intimate companions. Are they contented?

Devoe was not alone in his criticism of the newly formed
alternative prison system for children. William Sawyer, a
magistrate in Massachusetts, balked at sending children into
facilities that "make and increase the very evil they propose
to remedy." Ted Rubin, a Denver Juvenile Court Judge, made
essentially the same pronouncement some one hundred twenty-
five years later.

As bad institutions proliferated throughout the country, as
makeshift facilities and exploitative programs masked as reform moves began to settle into the rigid, mindless state institutions that would be on the scene for a hundred or more years,
there were still people who dreamed of ideal places for
children. "Log cabin" reform schools opened in Ohio and
"cottages" in other places. Edward Everett Hale, who wrote
"The Man Without a Country," wrote in 1855 in *Prize Essays
on Juvenile Delinquency* on the ideal conditions that the state
should consider in its plans for housing children without a
family.

> Wherever there are parents, incompetent to make their
> homes fit training places for their children, the State
> should be glad, should be eager, to undertake their care.
> Nay more, its own means for training those children must
> not be merely such as will suffice for the waifs and strays
> whom no one else shall care for. They must be so
> thorough and so successful, that parents shall not them-
> selves regret the care which is given to their children; and
> that, as often as possible, selfish and incompetent parents,
> too poor to educate their children well, may be willing to
> give them up to care which is so much better. The
> arrangements should be so wide, that the State should
> never refuse the care of children who may be offered to
> it by those who have them in charge. . . .

Hale's enthusiasm for these kinds of guilt- and stigma-free alternatives to one's family is similar to my best hopes for today. He went on to say that he believed his proposal was "not so Utopian." There, history and I part with him.

The state institutions that followed with the turn of the century offered little in the way of "thorough and successful" places for children. What the early 1900s did reflect was society's growing complexity and its tendency to corruption and gimmickry. School ships were tried in New York and elsewhere, in an attempt to "cast off" literally those whom history had cast off figuratively. On the positive side was the development of foster-home placement and the opening of a few places like the George Junior Republic in New York, which believed in hard work and self-determination, and the El Retiro School in Los Angeles County, where Miriam Van Waters created a "society of inmates" and emphasized group participation in government and self-expression in plays, essays, and a school newspaper. These efforts, by "Daddy" George and Dr. Van Waters, were uniquely personal efforts and went against the trend. Most institutions were moving toward the military school philosophy—increasingly the favorite solution to juvenile delinquency problems faced by the growing middle class and the rich. More and more private institutions began taking children from the courts, but they were, in the main, sectarian and selective. Few private institutions took black children. Most public institutions segregated them.

The Bridewell and the House of Refuge remained the models for state institutions for delinquent children, and also for the private institutions that were supported mostly by public money. They became so insular and self-serving that in 1898 the Society for the Prevention of Cruelty to Children refused to allow New York's State Board of Charities to inspect its facilities. It was ruled that since the SPCC was not a charitable institution within the meaning of the 1894 Constitution it was not subject to visitation. Ironically, an organization set up for "the Protection of Children" had won its battle to prevent a state board from protecting children *from them*. This set the stage for a "hands off" policy between regulatory agencies and juvenile institutions that is still in evidence today. The institutions that were set up or set themselves up to contain and control the children that nobody wanted were, on paper, responsible to state agencies. But the power and threat of these agencies scared no one.

Changes in juvenile court procedures during the 1920s and 1930s brought only token changes in the institutions that imprisoned children. The need and demand for increased rights and protections for children, pioneered and championed by such people as Jane Addams and Lillian Wald, did lead to reform through the courts, but ultimately the institutions and the courts themselves used these new "rights beyond the Constitution" granted to children to eliminate any constitutional protections for them. As usual, piecemeal reform of a bad system by cleaning up only one of its components was doomed to fail. The opportunities available within a society, the quality of life in it, the nature of families, the courts and institutions are all part of one picture. If history has taught us anything, it is that people have the capacity to change that whole picture. Or not.

Our Children's Keepers

1

New York

Youth House
Is Not
a Home

Youth House is a kid Big House for big and little kids. It is
a maximum security prison for children from six to sixteen,
mostly black and Puerto Rican, unfortunate enough to live
in a New York City slum. It destroys more children than any
disease, consuming some ten thousand each year, and escapes
periodic exposés of horror only to increase its destructiveness.
At a cost of more than $50 a day for each child, or $18,000 a
year, New York taxpayers are supporting one of the worst
children's prisons in the United States.

The history of Youth House begins in 1944, following the
Report to Mayor Fiorello H. LaGuardia made by a Committee of the Domestic Relations Court on the deplorable
conditions of the Shelter for Dependent, Neglected and Delinquent Children run by the New York Society for the Prevention of Cruelty to Children. The conditions exposed in
the La Guardia report included acute overcrowding, a

1

"barren, rigid routine," untrained personnel, and a total lack of recreational and psychiatric facilities. Discipline consisted of solitary confinement in a damp, rat- and roach-infested basement cell.

On April 3, 1944, Youth House was born out of a mixed marriage of private and public interests. Its $5,000,000 annual budget came equally from city and state funds, but its private Board of Directors was accountable only to itself.

From its opening to the early 1950s, through its expansion into girls' facilities in the Bronx, Youth House developed a reputation as a poorly equipped, understaffed dumping ground for delinquent and dependent children. The executive director during that period, Frank Cohen, fought impossible odds with the best of intentions. He wrote a report to his board of directors telling how kids had to go for weeks without recreation and "without getting any direct sunlight." He was optimistic, however, about the plans for a new building. "Since these plans for the construction of a central detention home are the first to be undertaken by the City of New York, it is hoped that the finished product will fully meet the standard of what an adequate detention setting should include and encompass . . . that it will be a facility evoking a sense of pride in all of the citizens of New York because of its forward-looking interest in behalf of children in trouble."

But while Cohen's optimism was not to be realized, his conclusion contained the key to understanding future rationalizations of failure: "however trying some of the steps in the Youth House development have been . . . whatever mistakes were made have been in behalf of the children we serve. . . ."

In December, 1957, the city opened the new Youth House for Boys on Spofford Avenue in the Bronx—a shiny, white, five-million-dollar monument to the low standards and poor judgment of New York's child-welfare experts. Nine days after it was opened the facility was obsolete, passing its 300-bed capacity by 25. According to the *World-Telegram and Sun,* July 9, 1958, "Long-range planners had figured in 1954 that the city's juvenile delinquency problem would level off in 1959 or 1960. So they designed the detention center with a capacity of 300 beds, 85 more than the accommodations at the old Youth House. . . ."

Following some changes in administration, the Youth House complex, now totally centralized in an inaccessible industrial section of the Bronx, settled down to a routine of chaos "in behalf of the children," keeping the tabloids full of stories of escapes, riots, death, and corruption. Reporting a typical "in-depth" analysis of the problem, the New York *Daily Mirror,* March 26, 1958, informed New Yorkers, "In the past three months 24 boys have escaped the city's Youth House at 1221 Spofford Avenue, Bronx, by picking locks. The latest two fugitives [sic], one 14, the other 13, fled yesterday.

"In an effort to do something about it, the Department of Public Works has been asked to make a study of the lock problem at the eight building institution. . . ." (Italics added.)

And as if the lock problem wasn't serious enough, only four days later the New York *Daily News* reported an even more serious problem with the sheets: "A 15 year-old boy died yesterday at Lincoln Hospital in the Bronx after falling from a third-story window in an attempted escape from Youth House. The dead boy . . . [had] tried to climb down two sheets knotted together but apparently they did not hold and he fell."

The reason given by the Youth House staff for the rash of violence and attempted escapes, wrote the *Daily News* in November, 1959, was the "permissive policy of the detention house authorities." By this time the escape total for the year had reached sixty-one. The *News* elaborated: "The guards claim that the boys, whose age alone prevents them from prosecution and jailing in harsher institutions, are coddled, even when it means over-riding the authority of their counselors and guards."

The children were hardly being coddled. At the Youth House for Girls, Manida, around the corner from the Spofford Avenue boys' facility, girls were sleeping on the floor or in the infirmary. Its absolute capacity, according to a study by the Children's Bureau of the Department of Health, Education and Welfare, was and still is 59 girls. But in a June, 1961, news item on a particularly violent riot, the New York *Journal American* quoted the assistant director of the home, Nathan Selden: "We have room for 105 girls, but there were 190 in it."

Youth House for Boys quickly went from its ninth-day over-capacity of 325 to 500, but "coddling" remained the number one explanation for the daily upheavals. No one, of course, was asking the kids.

Up to now the battle had been between the savage delinquent and the poor-but-dedicated social worker, the animal against the firm but understanding trainer. But in February, 1960, the real nature of the kid-coddlers on the Youth House staff began to surface. That month the Mackell-Brennan bill was introduced in the state legislature in Albany at the behest and with the support of the Youth House custodial staff. The measures would have classified the staff as "peace officers," made assaults on them assaults on an "officer," and permitted them to carry guns.

The *World-Telegram* (February 2, 1960) reported the custodial staff's position regarding their comparative discrimination:

> In support of the bill, an employee statement declared: "The odd thing in this whole situation is that a children's court probation officer who is basically a social worker is

a peace officer. A children's court officer whose duties are not near as involved with detention as ours, is a peace officer. An agent for the Society for the Prevention of Cruelty to Children, basically a social worker, also is a peace officer. Yet these custodial officers of Youth House are treated as second class citizens."

The Mackell-Brennan bill failed. But the orientation of the "basically social workers" was now clear.

My wife Michelle and I had heard about Youth House many times from the kids we knew and lived with at LEAP, an "intergeneracial" community we started on the Lower East Side late in 1962. Now a home, school, and family for more than a hundred people, young and old, black, brown, and white, LEAP began in a storefront staffed by Michelle and me in our "free time" each night and on weekends. Our main program, aside from the judo lessons that ostensibly brought us together with the kids, was talk. As trust developed, memories were disclosed: the thousand secrets each ghetto kid holds to himself or herself; the collective poison that prevents so many kids from ever wanting to live long enough to be grown up.

At first the stories came through in little edited blurbs, for the memories were too threatening. Then they flowed. Some kids told of recent recollections; only weeks had passed since their Youth House experience. Others had "long ago" experiences, three or four months old. Without exception the stories involved personal pain at the hands of the Youth House keepers. As adult members of this diverse community, LEAP, we decided to find out for ourselves what these people were doing to our kids and what we could do about it.

What had to hit anyone looking into Youth House was the fact that most of the children locked away there didn't belong locked up at all. While theft was a common complaint against many of the young inmates, it was nonetheless a *complaint* and not a conviction that had sent them there. After theft came truancy. The New York City Board of Education had one of the most efficient conduits into Youth House and regularly filled the courts and the Youth House rolls with its failures. The Board of Education, a parent, or a police officer could lock a kid up *on a complaint* without a formal remand, without ever facing a judge or seeing the inside of a courtroom. We learned of cases where children were held on such complaints for as long as a year without adjudication. And while many are held awaiting trial for such crimes as truancy or petty theft, others were simply dependent or neglected children or runaways—kids whose only crime was being born.

Only a small percentage—3 or 4 percent—could be considered "dangerous," most of them dangerous only to themselves, and this small minority needed specialized care which Youth House did not provide. Most experts, including the man who was executive director of Youth House when I first began my interest there, agreed. J. Martin Poland stated, while he was serving as the head of Youth House, that better than 90 percent of the kids locked up in the various Youth Houses didn't belong there. Their confinement to Youth House, made, according to New York State law, "in the interest of the child," was most usually related to their demeanor in the courtroom, their racial and class background, and the amount of adult support the children had. A poor black or Puerto Rican street kid on his own in Family Court, for whatever reason, could be fairly sure of a late afternoon ride on the blue and white bus marked "New York Bus Tours" that took kids from the court to Youth House each evening.

The recent Gault decision of the Supreme Court ruled, in effect, that kids have the protection of the Constitution. But the fact is that kids have no protection at all. They do not have equal rights to a speedy trial. They do not have the right to bail. In most cases a writ of habeas corpus would be laughed out of Family Court. Children may not be allowed to testify in their own behalf, lawyers are denied the right to cross-examine witnesses, and there are cases where a judge has actually denied counsel, preferring to run the entire hearing alone. Court procedures are almost totally arbitrary.

The arbitrary nature of trial and imprisonment and the corresponding lack of constitutional recourse did not turn out to be the most damning of LEAP's findings. Worse was the total lack of program, the absence of anything that might be considered "therapy," and the incompetence and brutality of the adult staff of Youth House itself. Beatings, forced homosexuality, and constant cruelty were the documented daily activities filling the program vacuum.

One young LEAP member, fifteen-year-old Felix Navarro, told of his experiences at Youth House, beginning when he was twelve years old:

> When I got to Youth House it was because my mother said I wasn't going to school. After a while I got a chance to work in the kitchen. On the first day, after I finished working, a guy who was on the staff for the kitchen was a gay and invited me to the back room so that we could fuck. . . . You know, have intercourse. I refused and asked to be sent back to my dormitory. He said if I didn't do it with him he would tell my supervisor that I was caught stealing and I wouldn't get fed. I told him, "I don't care, send me back to the dormitory." I was sent back and told my supervisor what happened. He laughed and told me I wasn't the first one.
>
> The next day I was walking through the hall and met four other inmates. They told me that for telling my supervisor what happened in the kitchen they had orders to beat me up. Then they took their belts off, wrapped them around their fists, and hit me with the buckles.

Felix finished his story slowly, then, as if remembering some small detail, added:

> Oh, yeah, one day I decided not to go to school . . . and so they told me I could stay in the dormitory if I cleaned the floors and walls. I said okay. Two other guys [inmates] were cleaning . . . with me. The three of us were told by Supervisor Poe to go into dormitory A4 and sit down. We did and another kid . . . a kid who was like . . . a faggot, he came in and pointed to my friend. Mr. Poe and another counselor told my friend to go into the other room and fuck with this kid. When my friend refused he was taken into the other room by the two supervisors. I could hear screaming and a lot of noise. It sounded like falling furniture. The counselors came out and told the faggot kid that he could go in, that my friend was ready for him. He went inside with the two supervisors following him. In a little while they all came out. Later my friend told me how he was forced to have sex with the faggot while the counselors were watching. They get a kick out of somebody going through it—then they make fun of him in front of everybody else.

Fifteen-year-old Patricia Shevack's memories of Youth House dated from when she was thirteen:

> There was only one good teacher, who was the typing teacher. We made all shapes of dolls on the typewriter and I asked her to teach me how to type but she said she could not do that. . . . I saw them beat up a girl twelve or thirteen years old because she took milk to her room for a cat. The supervisor beat her up, punched her and slapped her. . . . One day, in the shower, one of the girls got nasty and started feeling me and I told her off. I told the supervisor and she didn't do anything about it except take it out on me.

Armed with a collection of many such tales of "coddling" by the aspiring peace officers of Youth House, we contacted

James A. Wechsler, the editorial page editor of the *New York Post*, whose daily column is the only one available to the powerless of New York. Wechsler reacted to the matter-of-fact sincerity of the kids he heard with a series of columns. He concluded at the end of his initial two-day volley in the *New York Post:*

> Despite the inevitable resistance of vested interests and simple minds to any serious reforms, Deputy Mayor Costello's office, I learned yesterday, has been quietly exploring the sordid Youth House story . . . the Bronx District Attorney's Office is also preparing a report. . . .
>
> But no early miracle is likely unless legislative committees and other groups put the spotlight—and the heat —on Youth House, where children grow old and cynical too soon.

Less than one week later, on March 13, 1967, a state legislative investigation was under way. State Assemblyman Bertram Podell, Chairman of the Joint Legislative Committee on Penal Institutions, had responded to the Wechsler columns by making an unscheduled visit to Youth House and by personally interviewing ex-inmates and staff brought together by LEAP.

"I'm appalled and shocked," Podell told the *New York Post*, "that children who in many instances are guilty only of the crime of being homeless, parentless, or friendless are placed in an institution which is nothing more than a prison." Podell continued, "Children are being taken into custody and placed in this building of thousands of locked doors, without the slightest semblance of due process. A parent, policeman, or judge can throw these kids into Youth House where they are kept—often illegally—for periods ranging in excess of a year."

It seemed as though the word from the forgotten, battered kids inside the Youth House walls had gotten out. "It is apparent to me," Podell said after his Youth House tour, "that such detention prisons are nothing more than feeding grounds for our penal institutions. . . ."

His outrage had a faint echo. Nearly seven years earlier, in 1960, another State Assemblyman, Max M. Turshen, had told the *New York Post*: "These conditions [at Youth House] only contribute to delinquency. Unless the situation is corrected we run the risk of creating hardened criminals out of delinquents."

The risk, it was apparent, had been run. Now it was Podell's chance to bring the destructive Youth House saga to an end.

The Hearing Room in the State Office Building was filled with a curious assortment of people. The officials looked official and not terribly concerned. They had seen this all before. The one thing that seemed to put them off balance, to make them the slightest bit nervous, was the presence in this chamber of some thirty LEAP School kids who had taken this opportunity to see Democracy in Action.

To make matters worse, the kids were not overpolite; most were smoking and none wore a tie. Scattered through the room were past and present staff members of Youth House, eyeing each other suspiciously, wondering if anyone would risk telling the truth.

The kids told their stories. They were the now publicized documentaries of beatings and Oliver Twist-like backwardness. They were remarkably consistent—so much so that Wechsler was later to note:

> There were elders from Youth House and other involved institutions present who, while conceding that things were bad, preferred to believe that the recitals were "exaggerated." I must testify that there was no consequential discrepancy between the stories the kids told in my office and those they unfolded on the stand. . . .

Judith Andress, a twenty-eight-year-old ex-staff member, testified, "What the children have said here is true. . . . They are describing ordinary days at Youth House." She went on to describe the time when a Youth House counselor forced a young girl to "roll in her own urine" because she had become hysterical and wet her pants and the floor.

Another Youth House employee, twenty-six-year-old Elizabeth Annas, testified:

> Youth House was conducted like a prison. There was no attempt at therapy. I was told by my supervisor and people in personnel that the children were less than human and that they were animals. I was never to trust them or give them anything.
>
> I saw many instances where supervisors hit children with key chains and fists. Children were encouraged to fight each other and this was permitted by supervisors. . . . Children who couldn't speak English were abused by supervisors and in many cases their complaints not understood and disregarded.
>
> One girl about 15 years of age attempted to commit suicide twice and nothing was done to help her. It was only when she tried it a third time, when she drank a bottle of Clorox during visiting hours, that any attention was given her. . . .
>
> The important thing was not understaffing, which did exist, but the whole attitude of the administration who ran the institution like a penal institution. This attitude would have prevailed regardless of the number of children or number of staff.

A drama and music specialist at Youth House, Janet Rose, described her in-service training:

> On my second day at Youth House, I saw a young girl being beaten over the head with a chain by a supervisor because she refused to join with the other inmates in reciting the Lord's Prayer. . . . I learned that the girl followed the Religion of Islam. . . .

One teenage girl was beaten by a supervisor who [at a later point held the post of] Assistant Recreation Supervisor. The supervisor beat the girl with her shoe, kicked her and threw her to the floor, and beat her head on the floor. The child screamed for her mother, and the supervisor continued to beat her. I came to the child's assistance and got on top of her so the supervisor couldn't hit her anymore. . . .

Many other such statements from staff made it clear that either Youth House was indeed one of the most savage destroyers of children or there was under way in these hearings one of the best-rehearsed conspiracies in history. But if there were conspirators, the facts were to point away from the young inmates and disillusioned workers:

I went with Podell during the first of his prehearing visits to Youth House. Arthur Cole, Spofford's Director of Operations, nervously attempted to take us on the usual guided tour, an itinerary calculated to miss the highlights of Youth House life. But the kids had told us what to look for and despite heavy resistance we went our own way.

Chairman Podell was amazed at what he saw. Six- and seven-year-old boys were sobbing in corners while indifferent counselors looked on. These same children, wearing prison clothes, were pushed into line and forced to march, San Quentin style, through the halls to meals and "activities." When he finally spoke to one of the seven-year-olds and the sights and sounds became too much, Podell began to cry.

Each "off limits" corridor we went through buzzed with rumors and the sounds of interoffice telephones attempting to keep the staff prepared for our visit with as much notice as possible. We went into the pool room, which held about three or four pool tables and had room for perhaps sixteen kids. They had herded the big guys from the oldest dormitory into that activity when they found out we were looking for the oldest boys' quarters. There were about forty boys, mostly black, standing against the walls when we entered. Their counselor was lecturing to them in the high-pitched voice and affected posture of a drag queen. He screamed and pouted, hands on his hips, looked casually at us, and without warning pushed one of the smallest boys hard up against the wall. He decided who would play pool with whom. The biggest guys played. The others watched. Fights began among the spectators. The counselor screamed and twitted again, and this time the room exploded into violence. Kids were hitting each other with pool cues and fists, and throwing cue balls until reinforcements moved in. The violence stopped as quickly as it had begun. We walked out to see the "little kids" at a play period.

Walking through the hall, I noticed one of the smallest kids carrying what appeared to be a short truncheon, a club wrapped in tape and on a leather string. I called Podell over and he questioned the boy about it. The little boy was among the minority of white kids. He was seven and freckled and looked like a refugee from a Walt Disney movie.

"Hey, what's that thing you're carrying?"

"It's a club."

"What's it for?"

"Mr. Smith let me carry it."

"Oh. Well what's it for?"

"When we're bad, Mr. Smith hits us with it."

"Who's Mr. Smith?"

"He's our counselor."

"May I see it?" Podell took the club and, assuring the boy that he would not get into any trouble over its disappearance, put the club in his pocket. He warned the officials on our way out that he would be back to speak to the boy who had given him the club. He strongly advised them against harming him.

Back at the hearings, the last witness had testified. The attackers and the apologists had met in battle, and the weary committee members were about to begin sorting out the atrocities from the appeals for more money for more atrocities. They had suffered through a day of passion, horror, and white-wash with remarkably little emotion. A woman who looked like she was on a lunch break from the filming of *Oliver!* asked for the chairman's attention, and Podell recognized her.

"Mr. Podell, I wonder if you could give me little Ricky's drumstick back. He wants to play his steel drum tonight and you have has drumstick."

"He wants his *what*?" Podell answered in disbelief.

"He would like his drumstick back. He said you took it."

"You mean the club?"

"Oh, that's no club. That's Ricky's drumstick. He asked me to get it from you. Do you mind?"

"Yes, I do mind," Podell replied. "I do mind."

As it turned out, the boy confirmed it was a club, but truth in the hands of politicians is made of silly putty.

It came out in the hearings that Youth House had an officially sponsored youth Gestapo, a group of bully-boys established by the Spofford Avenue Youth House administration and called the Council. The "four other inmates" that Felix Navarro told us about, who beat him after he reported the homosexual advance of a Youth House staff member, were "Council boys."

The Youth House staff had always been sensitive to being called "guards." Although they fought for peace-officer status in the legislature, they somehow didn't want to carry the burden of a peace-officer-sounding title. So they were called "counselors." Now watch the spelling closely here.

In the post-hearing report issued by the Podell Committee,

a good portion of the violence at Youth House was blamed on "cadres . . . selected to assist staff members in maintaining order and discipline"—and these cadres were called "councilors" (quotes and spelling theirs). "Given some responsibility over the younger residents," the report went on, "these 'councilors' enforced discipline by systematic beatings of the youngsters entrusted to their charge."

Significantly, in an official Youth House document describing the Council program, the administration at no time used the word "councilor" in describing the Council members, while there are many references to "councilman" and "council boys." The document did make it clear, however, that while councilmen can assist staff with such routines as "distribution of linens, clean-up, and the orderly transit of groups from one area of the building to another, this is in no way intended to suggest that councilmen should be placed in authority over other boys."

In 1967 the Bronx Grand Jury issued a presentment on Youth House after one of these "Council boys" had killed another boy during one of these "orderly transits." The dead boy had broken the perfection of the rigid line of passage (called "boxing off"), was forced to endure a punch in the stomach (called "chesting") from his contemporary, and choked to death on his own vomit. The report of the Grand Jury indicted more than the "council boy" practice. But, as usual, it was to mean nothing.

And so there was violence, old against young, coupled with violence, young against young. But nowhere, before the Podell Report, was there any confusion about which was which. With a simple change of letters we were left to guess whether the "kown-sill-ors" responsible for those beatings, rapes, and urine-rollings were the kids or their keepers. And if semantic scapegoating wasn't sufficient to shift blame from where it belonged, the indomitable Youth House had another variety in reserve.

J. Martin Poland was the executive director of the Youth House complex at the time of the Podell hearings in March, 1967. He had been the head of Youth House since 1962, when he came up from Baltimore's correction system. At the same time John Wallace, also from the Baltimore system and an associate of Poland's, was made chief of the New York City Probation Department, which was to be the unofficial city agency "watching over" Youth House.

Poland's regime was marked by constant confrontations with his board of directors and City Hall over his public cries for detention reform. The Youth House board, selected by the mayor from lists provided by the Federation of Jewish Philanthropies, Catholic Charities, and the Federation of Protestant Welfare Agencies, thought Poland's public utterances put them in a bad position. They were constantly being forced to answer for the public charges of their own employee. The board's main concern, it appeared, was for peace and paper progress.

But Poland was a flamboyant man, not comfortable at peace. He was short, stocky, and exuberant, and looked more like a restaurateur than the administrator of a scandal-prone children's prison. He cared about kids, probably looking back at his own youth when he said, "I really understand these kids. I've been through a lot of the same things they have." He was a maverick and constantly risked his job by saying in public what the Youth House board of directors said only in private.

In short, J. Martin Poland was a perfect target. He had submitted his resignation to the board in September, 1966, but they did not accept it and asked him to stay until he could be replaced. He was a sitting duck.

Before Poland received word of the board's decision to accept his resignation, I had a chance to speak with him and get his feelings on the institution he had worked to reform.

Q. What do you think of Youth House?

Poland. I think it's an archaic service and should be done away with.

Q. Why don't you get support for change?

P. You're fighting the basic power structure. I don't even think most of these kids belong in juvenile court.

Q. But who wouldn't want to cooperate to change things?

P. Look, this strikes at everything . . . mostly the court system. I was asked what would be the greatest contribution I could make to child welfare in New York State. I said, "Burn down Youth House." Thereafter, I lived in fear that this would come back in an act of fate. I wish I could tear it down.

At this point he held up an article he had just published in a journal of the National Council on Crime and Delinquency. As an expert on youth detention, he had presented some well-founded suggestions for improved treatment.

P. Every time something like this comes out I get less powerful.

Q. Who takes the power?

P. It's very subtle. I'm at a cocktail party . . . and the Mayor's Administrative Assistant comes over to me and says, "The next time something like this happens, you're dead." The next thing you know, all my statements have to be cleared through all kinds of offices.

Poland continued by sadly reading portions of his letter of resignation:

> One criticism that has been legitimately leveled at Youth House, and one that we ourselves have made, is that we have failed to maintain minimum standards of good child care defined by the State Department of Social Welfare,

the National Council on Crime and Delinquency and the Federal Department of Health, Education and Welfare. . . . The court should not tolerate the overcrowding of a detention home. . . .

Administrators tolerate certain practices during periods of stress because if they did not we could not hold staff . . . we are chasing our tail. . . . There is no justification. . . . It is our responsibility to alter that situation.

We are often criticized for failure to meet standards for service breakdowns and for poor service. What hurts is that the criticism is valid. When we lose, so do thousands of children.

If the Board accepts my position, it has an obligation to take a firm position that will enable us to begin to do, in all our faults, the job we want to do. If the Board feels my position is impractical, untimely or invalid, the difference is so basic that in terms of rational integrity we should consider negotiating a separation.

Rational integrity. Whatever petty criticisms may have been made of J. Martin Poland, he had more of that than the "Blue Ribbon" board who hired him ("bought," as Poland put it) and then denied him the freedom to move.

Poland read one more line from his resignation letter: " 'We should refuse to accept pregnant girls until such time that we can provide the necessary care.' " He looked up. "Y'know," he said, "we have maintenance men delivering babies here."

The Podell hearings ended, and Poland disappeared as expected. People waited for the committee's report, although they knew what it would and would not say. It was clear that the committee would indict something or other. But what? And whom?

Salary limitations. They were to blame.

"Because of salary limitations," the report explained, "Youth House was unable to employ physicians and provided but limited nursing services. Based on uncontroverted evidence presented before the Committee, the conclusion is inevitable that medical services are virtually non-existent at Youth House."

It would be reasonable to assume that someone had something to do with these operational priorities. But there is a gentleman's agreement among politicians against making strong demands for personal accountability lest someone start making them accountable in return. "The system" is most easily condemned in these reports, since such condemnations really don't offend anybody in particular.

The report was myopic to absurdity when it noted without special comment, "Youth House has a capacity for 548 children and an operating staff which ranges from 550 to 650 persons." Aside from stating a capacity that is at least 250 kids higher than any other existing official study recommendation, the report confirms that while Youth House had better than a 1-to-1 staff-to-kid ratio, it was, through no fault of anyone's, prohibited *by its budget alone* from hiring a physician.

The report went on to condemn the fact that the public school at Youth House, a school run by the New York City Board of Education, had a space problem, "so that approximately half the children at Youth House cannot be admitted to the school." While admitting that a great many of the excluded half are in Youth House *because* of truancy, and calling that "indeed ironic," the report ventured into the reasons for truancy, since truancy, like the money that made doctors unavailable, was to blame for this enforced lack of education for so many kids.

"Many of the children," the report enlightened us, "are from broken homes where they have not experienced the daily discipline of a father going to work every morning, and consequently have not developed the disciplinary habit which deters truancy."

Disciplinary habits caused the truancy problem and the truancy problem caused the overcrowding. Untouched by human hands.

Nowhere is the Board of Education blamed for allowing such destructive "irony." The teachers' union, in all its concern for better conditions for teachers, shared none of this concern for kids locked *away* from school, and they weren't to blame either.

Nowhere was the Youth House board, in all its personal power and affluence, held personally responsible.

And nowhere was the Youth House administration held to account for its total abandonment of even the lowest professional standards for child care.

Nowhere were the Family Court judges blamed for their constant and flagrant breach of the law. According to many sworn statements, their act of remand, in those cases where a child did see a judge, in many instances actually contributed to the delinquency of minors. In many more instances, these judges, by their sentences to Youth House, prevented a child from attending school, which is a violation of the state compulsory education law.

And nowhere, but nowhere, was the mayor, under whose silver scepter all this was allowed.

The lack of discipline was to blame. Inferior locks and sheets that can't hold escapees.

Silly putty.

It was a game of musical blame and nobody lost but the kids.

Podell's vow to close Youth House, made only a few weeks earlier before the press and the cameras, his tears and his rage, were now only memories—dues paid for free TV time. In a political climate that was suddenly obsessed with law and order, the plight of the kids in Youth House, the kids past and the kids to come, had been reinterpreted. Podell announced his candidacy for Congress.

City Hall, in the meantime, responded to the pressures of the press by attempting to keep Mayor John Lindsay's shining armor from being tarnished until the whole thing could die down and be forgotten. The problems at Youth House, they would have had us believe, were merely sad remnants of New York's Wagnerian past. But exactly eight years earlier—after another period of scandal and reform—Mayor Wagner's office had issued a detailed report making many progressive recommendations.

Sixteen months had gone by since Lindsay took his oath of office, and his awareness of the Wagner report and interest in the kids locked away at Youth House, if either existed, had been a well-preserved secret. But everyone seemed willing to forget political motives and poor excuses. It seemed like the right time for action.

The city was working out the details to place the Youth House directly under city jurisdiction. Up until then it was a private corporation receiving its total support and referrals through the city and the state. New York City was, it said, moving to establish some firm accountability for what happened to its troubled kids.

James Wechsler, sustaining his commitment to justice in an unjust city, wrote in the April 24, 1967, *New York Post* about his visit to Youth House nearly a month after the Podell hearings. The date of the official city takeover was still under discussion. He described the "non-person" lives of the kids he saw there and the fact that the Youth House windows have not been able to be opened, even in the sweltering New York City summer, because "the keys had ceased to work many years ago." With characteristic optimism, he described his conversation with Simeon Golar, then Deputy City Administrator, the man given the task of saving-the-mayor-from-further-embarrassment:

> We rode downtown and Golar talked of the first steps that have been taken—such as the dismissal of some staff employees with crude criminal records. He was visibly angry and troubled. Youth House has long been run by a group of private citizens with City subsidy; now the City is at last moving in. But the problems remain deep, complex.
>
> Too many kids should never have been sent there; the wiser judges agree. . . . But many revolutions in attitude among many vested interests must still be overcome.
>
> Both Mayor Lindsay and Deputy Mayor Costello have apparently given Golar the signal to act on many fronts. He has the requisite qualities of spirit and imagination. For him the inmates are not to be viewed as "they" who are somehow unlike "we." But he has a long battle ahead.

Golar's battle lasted a few months. During that time he was able to force in the first regular medical program in the Youth House history and he got six- and seven-year-olds segregated from the bigger boys who may have been involved in more infectious destructiveness. He also managed to get the population down to 250. All of them were remarkable achievements. Golar was moved up to the New York City Housing Commission and soon after he was moved up again. He became Human Rights Commissioner. Over the period of his political ascendance, his interest in Youth House dwindled, Human Rights apparently being restricted to power groups older and more vocal than the kids locked away and forgotten in the Bronx.

In December, 1967, the City Council of the City of New York officially took over Youth House, placing it fully under the Department of Probation and John Wallace. Civil service arrangements for Youth House employees had still to be worked out, and it looked like there would be both the time and the motivation for Mayor Lindsay to sweep the place clean.

Wallace's first official act was to appoint Arthur Cole, the Director of Operations throughout Spofford's decline, as Director of Spofford. Outraged at such a flagrant betrayal of the spirit of the City Council's decision, various groups raised strong protests. The Citizens' Committee for Children, an important voice for liberal child-welfare legislation, opposed the appointment. In a letter to John Wallace, Trude Lash, the strength and creative force behind the CCC, expressed the Committee's opposition:

> Although we are not qualified to judge the character or merits of any particular staff member as an executive director, we have long believed that no one who has worked as a part of Youth House's detention system for a long period of time should be appointed director.
>
> It would be difficult for the public to believe that a new and clean administration has been instituted when a long time staff member of an institution with an unsavory reputation is promoted. I must confess that we too would have doubts.
>
> Therefore, we would urge that your new director be appointed from individuals unconnected with the detention system and thus free from the personal relationships that may make it difficult to transform the past detention system into one of which we can all be proud.

Almost every staff member who came forward to speak of Youth House spoke of Arthur Cole, and they did not speak kindly. They spoke of his bewildering immunity from the brush of reform that so often, however impermanently, painted out top administrators. And they spoke of the atmosphere of fear under which he kept silence and conformity among his staff.

Speaking for LEAP, I wrote to Wallace, Podell and Lindsay on January 3, 1968. I asked them to reconsider the appointment and continued in explanation:

> It is our position that [Arthur] Cole must not be permitted to serve in that capacity, since he served in the top managerial position during the years of Youth House's already established failure. As Director of Operations, Mr. Cole was [the administrative officer in charge of Spofford and therefore was] responsible for much of the chaos and destruction that appeared in the recent testimony. It would be a clear violation of responsibility to the community to allow him to continue, much less be promoted. . . .

John Wallace replied. He said he needed specific and detailed charges before he could terminate the employment of this dedicated public servant. I referred him to the thousands of pages of now-suppressed sworn testimony presented before Podell's committee.

Podell replied with the coolness that follows the heat of TV lights—"This will acknowledge receipt of your letter. . . . I have forwarded the correspondence"—only to warm up again when the TV cameras returned a little more than a year later, in July, 1969, when he testified on Youth House before the Senate's Subcommittee on Juvenile Delinquency.

John Lindsay did not reply, and what he lacked in concern he now bears in blame. Wallace named a figurehead replacement for Martin Poland as Executive Director, and gave Arthur Cole the job of Director of the Spofford Avenue Youth House, hereafter to be called—according to the city's public relations people and in classic Orwellian Newspeak—Spofford Juvenile Center. With one Executive Order, and as if by a wave from the 1984 model of the wand of Oz, Youth House ceased to exist. But life, for the now nearly six hundred kids locked up there each day, was not to be made better by the Lindsay-Wallace shell game.

By June, 1968, six months into total city control, Youth House had forgotten the reformers and was back in the routine of official malfeasance. According to staff members working there at that time, drugs were rampant at Spofford. Kids who were locked up for truancy or sassiness could whittle away the hours of boredom or escape the daily horrors in adaptive vocational training in the use of drugs.

The number of kids locked in Youth House continued on the rise as the fickleness of the press and public interest ran their downward course. By the end of 1968 Youth House was operating at twice its rated capacity, its program remained absent and undefined, and its staff was in even greater chaos than ever. A new staff member who quit just before Christmas in disgust after three days of Youth House routine reported his indoctrination.

"You see," said his supervisor, "this is supposed to be a non-punitive place. But the kids better not know it. Can you imagine if they knew it wasn't?"

"Did you ever hit one of them?" our informant asked.

"Everybody does. You've got to—you got to not be lax with them."

Late in the Spring of 1969, I called John Wallace and asked him if I could visit Youth House to see what, if any, progress had been made in the two years that had passed since the Podell hearing and during the year of city administration. He agreed to the visit, knowing that I could not be counted on as a Youth House partisan, and even agreed to show me around himself.

We pulled through the gates, past the security booth and into the lot reserved for the court bus and the cars of the top administration. We walked in the front door, past a few hard benches in the lobby, and were buzzed in through the main security door. I signed the log and began the walk down the corridor of offices and the large rooms, where new arrivals sat waiting to be processed.

Wallace had already prepared me for the worst. The place was jammed. The majority of kids locked up in the place weren't allowed to attend school. Many were being kept months after their sentencing to other institutions, and their months of waiting at Youth House did not count toward their "time". Psychotic kids were mingled with lost kids, kids with sexual problems mingled with truants. Big kids awaiting trial for murder sat confined with little kids awaiting trial for glue-sniffing. The windows were still stuck closed. For the perversely nostalgic, Youth House had remained free from the surrounding currents of change.

I thought of the months and years of struggle. Of the kids who suffered and never told. Of the Mayor's Phil Finkelstein, who dismissed the kids' testimony of suffering as "McCarthyism." Of the girl whose gang-bang rape in Youth House sent her into dope. Of Felix and Pat and Podell and tears and steel drumsticks and "councilors." All this in a flash as I noticed a group of adults in a circle, a little way down the hall, looking like a museum tour group. I asked Wallace who they were.

"Oh, they're new Family Court judges. We put them all through an orientation period here. We want them to know the whole picture of the place."

I stood for a moment and looked at them.

"Their teacher looks familiar," I noted with poorly hidden sarcasm.

"Oh, yes?" Wallace had moved quickly down the hall and away from the group. He waited for me to catch up.

I watched as the judges, following their teacher closely, tightroped the hallway, carefully avoiding body contact with the passing kids. Wallace unlocked another door and stood waiting for me to go through. I looked back again at the judges listening as Arthur Cole gave them "the whole picture."

On November 17, 1969, the New York *Daily News* began another exposé series on Youth House, calling it by its new name—Spofford Juvenile Center—and headlining drug traffic, sadism and "unnatural sex acts." Two state legislators promised a legislative hearing and the carousel music began again.

Epilogue

The *Daily News* series did lead to an investigation—indeed to three more in the next two years, and to the appointment of a "Blue Ribbon" panel to make "final" recommendations on the Youth House problem. Partially as a result of the recommendations of this Commission, the City of New York, once again, changed the titular management of the institution from one department to another. It would be transferred, according to Mayor Lindsay, to the Human Resources Administration, where "more humane solutions to the problem of neglected and abandoned children" could be found. The press and the public had, for once, united. And John Lindsay, then a presidential aspirant, looked as if he was listening.

I visited Youth House (now Spofford) late in 1971 with Stuart Black of the Institute for Juvenile Justice, who somehow managed to keep the spotlight on Youth House, despite a promiscuous legislature, for nearly five years, and Edward P. Morgan, the ABC correspondent who had, among his many other battles for social justice, initiated the now-legendary exposé of the treatment of migratory workers only a few miles from Youth House. We took the usual tour and things seemed pretty much as they did in 1967. They had added a medical facility and seemed justifiably proud of it. The rest of the place was in its usual state of neglect. It was still, despite mayoral pronouncements or aspirations, a class prison for children.

But it was in better hands. The man who had taken over control of all the city's detention centers for children was clearly the best hope yet. Wayne Mucci had tried to change the system in Connecticut and was "moved out" when his reforms threatened to disrupt the bureaucratic lawlessness. A new "law and order" governor swept Mucci out of office and the neanderthals breathed easy. Connecticut's perennial search for the seventeenth century inadvertently gave New York a chance to move into the twentieth. That is, if New York's own bureaucratic crazies didn't drive Mucci away again.

As we walked through, talking where we could with the young boys lined up in the halls, prison style, a staff member I knew came up to say hello.

"What do you think of the new takeover?" I asked him. "Do you think maybe this time it's for real?"

"Naw, hell, it's gonna be SOS. We all know it's gonna be SOS."

"SOS? What's SOS?" I asked.

"Same old shit," he answered, looking around to see who was watching him talk to me. "Guess who's Mucci's 'new' assistant? Arthur Cole," he said, and shook his head, and walked on past a line of seven- and eight-year-olds standing at attention.

Our friend was right. Arthur Cole was to be Mucci's assistant. But a few months later, for unexplained reasons, Cole was moved out. After long and painful discussions with LEAP, and with the Institute for Juvenile Justice, Mucci announced that the "worst" of the Bronx children's prison complex would be closed and that Spofford would be phased out within five years.

Victory had not yet come, rhetoric and reality being separated by the usual human factors. Like greed.

Employees' unions presently providing staff to "cover" kids at Youth House at almost a 2-to-1 ratio mobilized for an all-out fight. Construction unions, fearing that the new administration was going to delete a construction line in the city's capital budget, designated for a new two-hundred-bed girls' "shelter," lobbied and got a state senator to hold public hearings. Despite the fact that such construction clearly violated the trend toward smaller, more humane homes for homeless kids, they argued that "the state of the economy" made it necessary.

At last the real motives for the captivity of kids were surfacing. The economics of oppression were out in the open. It remained to be seen whether New Yorkers would continue to sell their children's futures so cheaply.

2

Denver

Portner's Complaint

"Hello, I'm Betty Portner. And this is Jerry Portner."

She was a big woman, large-boned, who looked about fifty-five or sixty and wore her hair piled on her head in the style of Joan Crawford. She sat behind her neatly ordered desk stiffly, welcoming me with a long silver letter opener. We did not shake hands.

I turned to meet Jerry Portner. I looked around the room and quickly looked around again. "And Jerry Portner?" I asked.

"Oh, yes, this is Jerry Portner." She pointed to the floor next to her desk. Jerry Portner was a large black poodle.

It was March of 1969 and I was at Mount View School for Girls, just outside of Denver in Morrison, Colorado, and Betty Portner was introducing me to the institution she had given nearly thirty-five years of her life to building and defending.

Miss Portner's was a civil servant's Horatio Alger story. She began at Mount View as an assistant house parent in 1934. From there she worked her way up to house parent, to bookkeeper, assistant superintendent and finally to superintendent. It was clear that her nearly thirty-five years of service had given her some sense that the school was her school. And it probably was. She also made it clear that she resented interference with her girls. I asked her what kind of rehabilitation program existed at Mount View, what kinds of treatment or therapy the girls were offered. It was one of many buttons I was to push that afternoon.

"Therapists. All they do is stir things up," she said. "They [the state] pushed in this group therapy just a little while ago and I'm telling you that it is just more trouble than it is worth. The nurse in one cottage tells me that the girls are in a state after that stuff. I'm gonna sit in on the next one and see just what the heck's going on in there . . . and if it's something that sets the girls off . . . well, that's gonna be the end of that.

"Now *I* have *all* the girls in the school for two hours *by myself* on Sunday, and if you ask me, we get down to cases and solve more things there than in any therapy."

"What do you do with the girls on Sunday?" I asked.

"Sunday, in chapel. I have the girls *by myself* for two hours every Sunday in chapel."

"What is the usual Sunday morning like? For instance, what would an average one be like . . . from the beginning?"

"Well, we start off by pledging allegiance to the Christian flag, and then the other one—you know, the American. We sing some hymns, and I read a portion out of the Bible and relate it to something going on in the school."

She gave me an example of group therapy Portner style.

A girl who had been at the school before and whom Miss Portner had identified as homosexual, was sent back to the school again on a wayward-minor petition. She had had a baby in the interim. When she came back, the girls who had known her before approached her with a sexual invitation, which she turned down. Betty Portner's triumph came when this girl stood up in chapel and confronted her rejected lovers.

"'Now look, you punks,'" Portner proudly related the girl's speech, "'I have a baby now and I've been through all that stuff. I've made my mistakes but now I've learned and you should just grow up and stop acting so dumb.'"

A Sunday-morning chapel cure. And who's to tell? After all, isn't it the goal of these places just to change *behavior?* But I was there to see the school, so I asked if we could get on with our visit.

Miss Portner's mood seemed to change. "Just what do you want to see?" she asked. "Just what are you looking for?"

"Well, for one," I said, hoping to put her at ease, "I'm interested in innovation. Every school of this kind seems to have something going on that may be of interest to others. Your chapel program, for instance."

"Innovation huh?" she said. "Well, there's no point in looking around here then, because we don't have any."

Stumped. "Well why don't we just look around anyway?" I offered, and we went out of her office and onto the campus.

The first building was only a hundred yards or so away, but Miss Portner, followed dutifully by Jerry Portner and me, chose to drive. We got into her Lincoln Continental and drove the few seconds it took to reach the chapel, our first stop.

Betty Portner had built the chapel. It was her ultimate accomplishment. The State of Colorado couldn't put up the money for the construction of a Christian chapel ("we haven't had a Jewish girl here but once and that was thirty-four years ago"), so "we built this chapel with the money from people I went to in Denver. It was twenty-five dollars a window," she said, pointing to the small rectangular colored windows in the brick, glass, and wood hexagonal structure, "and five hundred dollars a pew."

"And this is where you hold forth on Sunday?"

"This is where I hold forth."

"Is there a regular minister for the girls?" I asked, not knowing I had pushed Button Two.

She went into a rage about the minister. "I was just livid. . . . It was Easter Sunday and do you know that he came down off the pulpit and right down on the level with the girls and started talking about some movie he had shown on Wednesday night where *Christ*, mind you, was some sort of puppet or a clown. Well, let me tell you I was livid and I said, 'Now just what's going on here anyway?' I think he is just too far out. He says the smallest part of his concern here is what happens on Sunday. Can you imagine that?"

This wasn't Miss Portner's only problem with clergymen. A Catholic priest who had recently left Mount View also drew her fire. "He didn't belong in a school for girls, if you know what I mean."

We got back into the Lincoln and drove the next two hundred yards to the school itself. On the way I asked her about its racial composition. Button Three.

"You know, the colored used to be much easier to deal with. But since all that civil rights stuff, we're beginning to have trouble with them in here too. They just keep pushing further and further. Once you give in to one thing, then they expect that as if they always had it coming, and what you used to give out as a privilege becomes something they just take for granted.

"We had a colored man working here. He was our psychologist. And do you know, you couldn't even tell he was colored. Everybody just loved him."

I asked again about the racial makeup of the school; it turned out that about 75 percent of the girls were black or Chicano. As we sat in the car, now parked in front of the school, she prepared me for the visit.

"I think the most important thing to these girls is appearances. How somebody looks or something looks. If someone is neat and clean and dresses well, the girls respect them. Now our principal, he's a colored man. And that's OK but he just looks bad. He dresses sloppy and sometimes I'm just so embarrassed for him I can't stand it."

We entered the school and went into a class that was in session. All the girls snapped to attention when Miss Portner walked in. The teacher was moving nervously between the kids and Miss Portner.

Ironically, we had walked in on a discussion of racial identity. Miss Portner asked the class to continue what it had been doing before she came in, and the kids quickly got back into their discussion.

A Chicano girl began, "I never used to know how to act. Whether to act like Spanish or try to be Anglo."

The teacher, a black woman in her middle or late forties, answered what hadn't been a question. "I think you should just be yourself, what you want to be."

A beautiful black girl with a wild afro answered in the deepest anger.

"You can't be what you want to be unless you got somebody to back you up."

"Now girls," said the teacher, "you keep talking about being this or that—that's how you got in here. And if you want to make it out, you gotta learn how to be young *American* girls and not all this racial stuff. You understand?"

The anger on the little girl's face never faded. Her name is Lillian.

The teacher thought she would get us into the discussion and so she asked me what I thought about "this racial stuff." Before I could answer, one of the girls asked me where I was from. I told them I was from New York.

"Did you ever meet Bobby Kennedy?" she asked.

"Yes I did."

"Did you know him?"

"Yes, I knew him."

"Well, what would hea' said about this?"

"I think he would say that you should always be proud of whatever you are, because that's what you've really got to back you up."

Lillian showed a little smile, and I winked back.

I was afraid my subversive platitude might have meant the end of my visit. But Miss Portner only smiled and led the way out of the class.

We were on our way to visit the Principal.

"He's just not right here. You'll see what I mean," she said straightforwardly. "I've tried everything to get him out but I haven't been able to. I guess I'll just have to wait it out."

The Principal was a black man in his late forties who seemed at home in an institution—not one to offer up anything particularly exciting, and in this way fitting in well with Miss Portner's concept of the school. He seemed to be motivated most of all by a search for placidity. He looked tired.

I asked him about Lillian.

"Oh, her. She's just trouble, nothin' but one kind of trouble after another."

"But she seems so bright," I said.

"I guess so," he answered, "but she sure is trouble."

We exchanged a few minutes of school talk and Miss Portner and I walked into another class. The kids jumped to attention, we visited a few minutes, and we left.

Back into the Lincoln with Jerry and Betty Portner, past Portner Hall, and over to Taylor Hall for lunch. Portner and Taylor are ultra-modern buildings; Taylor has a central recreational and dining area, with living units in wing design surrounding the central area—a nice facility that looked like a modern college dormitory and lacked the oppressiveness typical of youth institutions.

I introduced myself to the girls and the staff and we sat down to wait for lunch. Betty Portner was snapping her fingers to the beat of the Mantovanni-type Muzak, obviously not of the girls' choosing, coming over the speaker in the dining room.

"That's my kind of music," Miss Portner answered clairvoyantly.

"What's a day's schedule like here at Mount View?" I asked one of the girls at the table.

The girl looked over at Miss Portner, who nodded her approval. This was the schedule:

> Up at 6:30
> Bathe
> Clean rooms
> Breakfast
> Clean
> School
> Lunch
> Clean
> School
> Bathe
> Clean
> Choir
> Sleep

"You must major in being clean," I joked. No response.

"Appearances are very important," Miss Portner said finally. "Let me tell you how important. One day some girls showed up in Chapel in work dresses. Can you imagine that? They just came right from work in their work clothes and I really let them have it. One of them was a Mexican girl, and she was in here for being part of that riot at West High School. (Would you believe she's been trying to *organize* the girls?) Anyway, I let them have it. I said, '*Some* people in this school are trying to make the whole student body look bad by disgracing our school' "—a junior high school band, Miss Portner told me, was coming to play at the school, and she wanted to make a good impression—" 'Well, *no one* is going to meet anyone from outside until you all look decent.' And do you know, the girls applauded? And they went out and came back in and every one of them was dressed and spotless and I stood at the door and checked every one of them myself."

Lunch arrived, and we ate quietly. When we had finished, Miss Portner and I reentered her car. I asked her why only one of the thirty girls in the "special unit" we had just visited was black. It turned out that most of the black girls were in a dilapidated building on the other side, a building that we passed by but that I was not allowed to visit. "It was built in 1913, and we really need to condemn it."

As we again pulled to a stop in front of her office, she told me that a sociology professor, Dr. Barber, from Colorado University, sends girls from his sociology class down to act as sisters to the girls. "We do have some sort of innovation, I guess," she said, "after all. We get as many as ninety girls coming in here twice a year. They come at least six times and take the girls out. It's more like a peer relationship—like with a sister, where with us it's more like a mother or grandmother. They go off campus horseback-riding and all that and they go unescorted."

I was surprised at the openness of that. But my surprise was short lived.

"The [college] girls have to write a report on each six visits and some of them even come more often."

"Who sees the reports?" I asked. "Do you get copies?"

"Oh my, yes. We find out a lot of valuable things that we otherwise would never find out. You know, they tell these girls things they would never tell us. And we have to find a way to deal with what we find out in this way that doesn't ever let the [Mount View] girls know how we found out. Otherwise we'd lose these college girls as a source of information.

"Anything else you'd like to know?"

"Yes. What about punishment? I've heard rumors that you use solitary confinement and physical punishment for misbehavior and running away."

Miss Portner studied me hard. "Look. These girls are in here because they broke the rules of society and if they can't take what we're dishing out then it's just too bad."

What about more active citizen involvement in youth institutions?

"They should leave decisions to the people who run these places. They took away a psychiatrist we had who gave us twenty hours a week and gave us a psychiatric team for one day a week for that money. And *they're* the ones who started all this group therapy and all the trouble we're having now with that; you know—they call anything progress."

She went into a story about a girl who complained in her cosmetology course about not having enough supplies and how another girl said, " 'How dare you complain about that? When you came here you didn't even have your own brush and now you have the nerve to complain about not having a certain makeup.' And do you know," Betty Portner added, "all the girls stood up and applauded. Now *that's* what I call therapy. Not all this shaking the girls up for days afterward. I just wonder what goes on in there for them, shaking things up so badly."

What about visits from family?

"One hour a week visit from parents if parents live less than twenty-five miles away, two hours a week if they live more than twenty-five miles away."

Visits home?

"We give girls weekend passes after five months and we've only had four run away and none of these has come back pregnant. We can't let a lot of them go home because, well, you know, we tell them, 'Now what do you want to do? You know you can't go home because when you were there your father played around with you. So what do you want to do?' And do you know?—A lot of them say that they want to stay here."

This wasn't the first time she'd rung a bell that sounded like man-hate, so I asked her if the students were permitted contact with boys. Letters? Visits?

The girls weren't allowed to get or send letters to boys, and no visits were allowed. But changes in these rules were being discussed.

Might this isolation from boys force girls into homosexuality who otherwise might prefer to be heterosexual?

No.

What about access to the news, or to radio and television?

One dormitory has transistor radios and can use them two hours a week.

Runaways?

"One year is added to the sentence of anyone who tries to run away."

I got out of the car and extended my hand to say good-by.

"Is there anything you would like to add that I didn't ask about?" I asked her.

She took my hand.

"I'm just a down-to-earth person. I don't know much about all this therapy stuff. I do know that these so-called professionals make a lot of trouble trying their 'far out' stuff. And we don't like any 'far out' things here."

But like it or not, admit it or not, Betty Portner *did* have some far-out things going on at Mount View. There were a lot of people around who did not applaud them.

In 1968, several employees and ex-employees concerned about conditions at Mount View and about their own treatment there gave testimony to the attorney for the Colorado State Civil Service Employees Union about their experiences and suspicions. These affidavits were taken by the union and forwarded to various state officials responsible for children's institutions in Colorado.

Father Knapp was one who testified. He had specific objections to the school's use of a solitary confinement cell called, in keeping with kid jail Newspeak, the Rose Room. That was only the beginning of his objections to the treatment of girls at Mount View. In his statement, Father Knapp, a Roman Catholic priest of the Franciscan Order, gave the following testimony:

> It is my opinion that the School is repressive in nature; that the School officials take a very negative attitude toward sex; that healthy friendships are not allowed; that an unhealthful attitude has been taken toward the male sex. Specifically, no pictures of boys—even brothers—are permitted. No letters to boys are permitted with the exception of one which is to say that such letter writing is not permitted. A suspicious attitude is fostered concerning the male sex by some of the higher staff members. Also the girls are not allowed to see newspapers, or to listen to the radio broadcasts. As a resut, they are completely out of touch with reality.

The theme of sexual repressiveness and a conditioning to guilt and fear in relation to members of the opposite sex came up many times in my discussions and investigations of Mount View. But Father Knapp's tale of the ash pretty much sums it up.

He was, along with the Protestant chaplain, conducting an Ash Wednesday service for the girls. Some of the ashes he was placing on the forehead of one of the girls fell down onto her nose. He took his finger and brushed the ashes off the girl's nose and, at the same time, commented, "Now you have a dirty nose." Miss Portner became "livid with anger as a result of this physical contact. . . ."

Father Knapp also was highly critical of the practice of depriving the girls of information concerning the world outside. Noting that he was at the school on the day following Martin Luther King's murder, he recalled talking to one of the black girls and expressing his regret that Dr. King had been killed. The girl, it turned out, knew nothing of the incident. Nor, Father Knapp found, did any of the girls in the school. Miss Portner's explanation was that she didn't want them upset by such news.

Father Knapp had another opinion of Miss Portner's favorite therapist, the one she had discussed with me who was replaced by this meddling psychiatric team who was "stirring up things." Said the priest of the therapist, "I very much doubted Dr. Stephenson's effectiveness, because about the extent of his contact with the girls was a short interview in their rooms and the prescription of sedatives. . . ." Father Knapp stated that most of the girls at the school were kept heavily sedated. He was happy that Dr. Stephenson had left the school and felt that the new psychiatric team was "progressive, realistic, and fully intended to institute broad changes."

Finally, Father Knapp thought that the administration actively fostered the idea among the girls that men want only sex from them and should always be held suspect. Along with the rather negative references to heterosexuality, he believed that Miss Portner and her chief aide, Mrs. Culpepper, were at the same time obsessed with a morbid fear of homosexuality at the school. As a result, the rules and regulations they instituted rigidly restricted friendships and personal relationships among the girls. "Any physical contact of any nature is immediately interpreted as homosexual activity," he explained, and, as a result of these restrictions, "the girls are starved for any sort of personal relationships."

In what might be a logical conclusion to the building up of such pressures and back pressures, Father Knapp, finding the girls "absolutely not prepared to meet the challenge and obligations of society once they are released," spoke of a "criminal organization which works out of Colorado Springs and Pueblo. It is aware of the status of the girls when they are released from the school, makes contact with them, utilizing the girls for both dope and prostitution purposes." He did not know any specific details concerning the operation of this group, but it had come to his attention on "a number of occasions," and he did not doubt its existence.

Neither, in fact, did Dr. Jerome Schulte, a former psychiatrist at Mount View who, according to the statements of Joe Pipa, a teacher there since 1967, called him to his office two or three weeks after he had begun teaching at the school. He was invited to the Clinical Services Division along with another teacher for a conference with Dr. Schulte, who immediately began to warn him and the other teacher about what he called "the syndicate" existing in the school. Dr. Schulte stated that some teachers in the school were members of this syndicate and that it was "extremely well organized."

"Specifically," according to Pipa, "Dr. Schulte stated that the syndicate had such power that it could arrange with the courts to have girls committed to the school. Once they were admitted to the school, they were instructed in matters pertaining to dope and prostitution and then, when they were released from the school, they were immediately placed within the syndicate for purposes of dope and prostitution." According to Pipa, Dr. Schulte told him that "this syndicate included people to the highest levels of the state government."

But Pipa was never able to substantiate Dr. Schulte's allegations. Dr. Schulte left Mount View soon after his meeting with Pipa and there were rumors that he had been threatened and that an attempt had been made on his life. Father Knapp left, too. According to a member of his order, one day he "just signed out and didn't come back."

Again, as with so many other kid jails, there was a pattern emerging. A pattern, at best, of improper treatment and inadequate care for kids, one that strongly suggested something pathological, insidious, and intentional. Why would a teacher, a priest, and a psychiatrist suggest that organized crime was involved in the operation of a state school for girls? Why, since these allegations and more had been presented all the way up to the governor of the state, had they been ignored for so long? Was this just the usual bureaucratic bungling and institutional character disorder, or was this something else?

When it came to institutional racism, there was no bungling at all. As the facts unfolded, it became apparent that there was a clear and organized policy to keep blacks out. Jews seemed to be similarly excluded.

Here, I think, Dorothy Jensen's affidavit should speak for itself:

> My name is Dorothy Jensen. . . . I work at the Mount View Girls School and began working there in June, 1966. I am a principal clerk-steno, and am presently working as secretary to Mrs. Mary Lou Culpepper who is the supervisor of the Group Living Department.
>
> One of Mrs. Culpepper's duties is to interview applicants for positions at the Mount View Girls School. Prior to a change that was instituted in the later months of 1967 . . . the following procedure was followed with reference to

applicants. An applicant would first come to my desk and I would give her an application. She would fill it out and then she was interviewed by Mrs. Culpepper. If Mrs. Culpepper didn't like the applicant, the application would be returned to my desk. Usually there would be a note attached to the application with some handwritten remark on it. I would file these applications in the file drawer.

During the summer of 1967 . . . I asked Mrs. Culpepper if it would be all right to clean out the Application File. She said, "Yes," and not to keep any applications that were older than six months. This I did, and threw away approximately three hundred applications. These dated back as far as 1964 and some had been handled by Mrs. Culpepper's predecessor, Miss Sweeten. Almost all of these applications had remarks attached to them. Many of them pertained to the personal appearance of the applicant. A substantial number of them—at least fifty—had the remark "colored" or "Negro" attached to them. One had "Jewish" attached. All of these with notations of "colored," "Negro," or "Jewish" also had the word "no" written on them.

During the time that I have worked for Mrs. Culpepper, there has only been one Negro employed. I would estimate that there have been at least thirty Negroes apply. The Negro who was hired applied during June, 1967. . . . She had already been certified by the Civil Service Commission and was sent to Mrs. Culpepper for an interview. Her name is Flora Campbell. She was about twenty-one years old.

After Flora had been interviewed by Mrs. Culpepper, Mrs. Culpepper made the statement in the presence of Mrs. [Jean] Reeb and myself that she wasn't "going to have a nigger" working for her. Mrs. Culpepper then told me to write a letter to the Civil Service requesting that they set a minimum age of twenty-five, because, in that way, they wouldn't have to hire Flora. I did write this letter. Later Mrs. Culpepper was called by Mr. Mylton Kennedy of the Youth Services Division of the Department of Institutions, and told to hire Flora immediately. Consequently she was hired.

. . . I have seen Mrs. Culpepper write remarks such as those above on notes that were attached to the applications. I am not aware of anyone telling her to write such remarks. I do know that Miss Sweeten apparently did the same thing.

The change referred to in the later part of 1967 is that the Civil Service now requires Mrs. Culpepper to send a copy of *every* application to them. To my knowledge, this is being done. Before this change the only applications that were filed with Civil Service were those that were filed by persons who were hired.

The State Civil Service Employees Association subsequently took the applications with racial notations described by Mrs. Jensen to a qualified expert in documents and handwriting. The bulk of them were identified as having been written by Mrs. Mary Lou Culpepper.

The black principal of the school—the one Betty Portner described to me as "not right here . . . you'll see what I mean" —is Lawrence Lewis, and his fatigue the day I met him became more than reasonable as I found out more about the pressures he faced.

His credentials read more like those of a private-school headmaster than those of the principal of a state school for girls. He had a Bachelor's and a Master's degree and had done advanced work at the Universities of Oklahoma and Colorado. He had attended De Paul University in Chicago. He taught in the public schools from 1950 to 1957 as an elementary principal, assistant high school principal and basketball coach. He taught in the Denver public schools and at the state reformatory at Buena Vista for two years. A veteran of World War II, he had received five battle stars in the European theater.

But he wasn't good enough for Mount View:

While I was teaching at Buena Vista, a notice in the paper was brought to my attention with reference to the hiring of teachers at the Mount View Girls School. I immediately made a phone call to the school about the job. I was asked to give them my application, and was asked my name, address, experience, and nationality. I gave them this information, and when I said, "Negro," they said, "That's enough, we'll let you know." I never heard further, until I wrote to the school inquiring about my application. I received a letter back from Miss Portner saying the position had been filled.

A few months later, I saw a Civil Service Notice announcing an exam for principals. I took the exam and passed. I placed first in the teacher's tests and second on the principal's test.

In August, while on vacation, I was called by Civil Service and told there was a vacancy at Mount View Girls School and that I should call Miss Portner for an interview. I did call, and told them who I was and why I called. The answer was to the effect that there was no vacancy in the principal's position. As I agreed to do, I called Civil Service back. They said they knew there was a vacancy and said they would contact me again. A few minutes later Civil Service called me back and told me they had made an appointment with Miss Portner for a few days later.

So I went out to the school for the appointment and was interviewed by Miss Portner. One of her first questions was, "Tell me about yourself." This I did. She brought up the fact that there were a number of girls at the school who were white and who "loved Negro men," and that this could be embarrassing for me. She explained how they manipulated the situation with resulting embarrassment. I told her I was happily married and I could not see how this would be a problem for me. Miss Portner said, "I am not prejudiced, but I believe in black marrying black and white marrying white." After further discussion along these lines, she said she would let me know about the job.

A few days later I called her about the job, and she said she hadn't made up her mind but would let me know in a few days. When I next called, she said I had been hired, and I was to report the following Monday, which was August 26, 1960. I have been working in the position ever since.

The evidence of racism piled up. Mrs. Jensen said that Mrs. Culpepper frequently referred to blacks as "niggers" and made derogatory comments about some of the black residents, calling one rather large black girl a "Black Mammy," for example.

Jean Reeb, a former employee of the school, testified that Mrs. Culpepper had once demanded that a girl runaway, who had been brought back to Colorado from Georgia "so weak she could hardly walk," be handcuffed for the trip to Colorado General Hospital because "the little black bitch will never get away from *me*." Mr. Lewis, according to Mrs. Reeb, was, in Mrs. Culpepper's eyes, "that black son-of-a-bitch," especially after he had been cleared of charges brought against him by one of the girls—charges she had been hoping would stick. Another time Mrs. Culpepper left orders that "no Negroes were ever to use the bathroom in the office," after a black student working in the office tried to use a nearby bathroom.

As for the Civil Service Commission "changes" Dorothy Jensen spoke of, making it a rule that *all* applications for employment be submitted to them and not just those who were hired, Mrs. Reeb told how that was bypassed by Mrs. Culpepper. Where before the applications used to note the race of the racially rejected applicant, now the applications were destroyed, making it impossible for the Civil Service Commission or anyone else to detect racial bias in hiring.

Jeanne Dotson, a Registered Nurse at Mount View from 1967 to 1968, filled in some more of the sharpening picture. She told of how she saw the school damaging the lives of its girls. She described the regular admission procedure followed for every girl who entered Mount View, a procedure that seemed calculated to frighten an otherwise disoriented person into hysteria.

> When a girl came to the school, she was met by a nurse at the Hospital Cottage. She was completely undressed, and all personal possessions were taken from her. Then, each girl received a shampoo and bornate treatment, which is a disinfecting process. This was done in a back porch of the cottage where the laundry facilities were kept. There were girls, staff members, and occasionally maintenance men walking about. There was no privacy for the disrobed girls here.
>
> Once this step was completed, the girl was given a muslin gown and directed to walk down the hall to the bathroom. There, they were required to take a bath under the observation of a nurse. After the bath is completed, they brush their teeth, and are given a clean robe and socks and necessary personal items for female hygiene.
>
> Then the girl is taken to the hospital examining room . . . given a questionnaire regarding their personal medical and social history . . . a list of rules and regulations . . . and interviewed by a nurse.
>
> Then the girl is locked in her room for a period of seven days, at a minimum, depending on her conduct. During this period she is not permitted to have any contact with any of the other girls. . . .
>
> This isolation period was used for health reasons and to cause the girls to give thought to her situation.

Mrs. Dotson, as the school's Registered Nurse, personally observed girls in the Rose Room, the school's solitary confinement cell. One such girl, whom I shall call Tina, had been locked in her room and had her windows boarded up after some kind of incident in the cottage kitchen. Mrs. Culpepper caught her trying to pry the boards loose from her windows and had her locked in the Rose Room. Mrs. Dotson said, "Tina was put into the Rose Room and began pounding on the door so violently that it was necessary to have one of the maintenance men bar the door with a two-by-four plank. I called the psychiatrist and requested that he authorize a sedative, but he wasn't available."

When Mrs. Dotson returned to the Rose Room, other staff members were present and were trying to put handcuffs on Tina. After they got the handcuffs on her, Tina's legs were tied behind her and fastened to the handcuffs—hogtied.

"Somehow," Mrs. Dotson went on, "Tina was able to turn the water on in her room, and as a result flooded the floor. She was still handcuffed, and obviously could not walk. Mrs. Culpepper was consulted and she stated that they were to let Tina lie in the water in the bottom of the room. She was left laying in the water for several hours."

Then Mrs. Dotson said something that was to be said again by other people at other times. She said that Mrs. Culpepper appeared to get "some sort of personal pleasure from physical contact with the girls," and recalled one evening when a girl was taken from a cottage to the Rose Room. After supervising the transfer and physically locking the girl into the solitary cell, Mrs. Culpepper commented that she didn't mind that her husband wouldn't be coming over to sleep at the school with her that evening, because she would "get her kicks" this way.

Jean Reeb corroborated nurse Dotson's allegations. An affidavit from the Civil Service union reads, "Jean stated that it is quite obvious that Mrs. Culpepper derives sadistic pleasures from such physical encounters with the girls. In fact, she has repeatedly made such statements after such occurrences as, 'Well, I've gotten my kicks for the day.' In fact she once stated . . . that she gets greater pleasure out of such encounters than she does from an act of sexual intercourse."

Jean Reeb also had a lot to say about the lives of the girls she worked with at Mount View, and like nurse Dotson her worst memories centered around the Rose Room. She gave me four cases that she thought presented a true picture of the treatment conditions the girls found at Mount View. What follows are those brief histories, just as Mrs. Reeb presented them. I have changed the names of the children.

Patricia Herrerra

"Patricia was a very ornery girl and was continually causing trouble. As a result, Mrs. Culpepper disliked her, and she was confined in the Rose Room at Mrs. Culpepper's direction. She remained in the Rose Room for eighty-one days before Mrs. Culpepper would give her permission for Patricia to be released from the room. As a result of this confinement, Patricia became psychotic and was taken to the Colorado Psychopathic Hospital in Pueblo."

Terry Ephron

"Around Christmas of 1967, Terry and [another girl] ran away from the school. A couple of days later they were picked up and brought back. Miss Portner told me that she was to be confined in the Rose Room. I asked her how long she was to stay in the Rose Room, as was my custom since it is rather common for girls to be confined for extended lengths of time in the room. In response to my question, Miss Portner stated, 'I don't care if she never gets out.'

"Terry was confined in the Rose Room for approximately forty-five days. During her confinement it became obvious that she was suffering from a mental disorder. As a result, we took her to the Colorado Psychopathic Hospital in Pueblo. I later determined that Terry's parents had not been advised of their daughter's removal from the school to the Psychopathic Hospital. This was not uncommon, since Mrs. Culpepper and Mrs. Portner take the attitude that they do not have any obligation to keep the parents or guardians of a girl advised of what happens to her during her confinement at the school."

Lola Grimes

"Lola, prior to her admission to the school, was apparently a heavy user of drugs, both narcotics and LSD. Shortly after her admission to the school, she was transferred to the Colorado General Hospital in Denver because of her deteriorated physical condition. It was there determined that she is a victim of chronic hepatitis. She is extremely excitable physically, and the nurses of the Hospital Cottage have noticed that as soon as she becomes excited in any way, her pulse becomes extraordinarily rapid. As a result, the nurses fear that such excitement could result in immediate death. Consequently, they have conferred with a doctor at the State Hospital in Fort Logan, with reference to the administering of any further drugs. He has advised that no medicine is to be given to Lola until he is able to thoroughly become acquainted with her case.

"However, upon Lola's return from Colorado General Hospital, she was immediately confined to the Rose Room. I have talked to Lola at some length and have formed the opinion that she is both physically and mentally very sick. Occasionally, she has screaming fits, which she describes following those fits as 'freak-outs.' Lola explains these as being a direct result of her previous use of drugs (probably LSD). Neither the nurses nor I believe that she is faking these so-called freak-outs. In addition to her other problems, Lola has suicidal tendencies and has tried to commit suicide on different occasions at the school.

"Recently, Lola was having one of her freak-outs and the nurse on duty called Mrs. Culpepper who came over to the Hospital Cottage. She went into the Rose Room where Lola was screaming and yelled at her that 'this had gone far enough.' She was still screaming, so Mrs. Culpepper grabbed her by the hair on the back of her head, and very forcibly pushed her face into the mattress and rubbed her face back and forth screaming at her that she had to quit yelling.

"Mrs. Culpepper left orders that Lola is not to be released from the Rose Room until she personally approves such release."

Debby Carson

"This was another incident where the girl was misbehaving and Mrs. Culpepper called me and asked me to go to the Rose Room with her. She told her that Debby would have to be placed in restraints. This means that it was necessary to handcuff her and otherwise restrain her physically. After this was accomplished, Debby was still belligerent and Mrs. Culpepper forced her down on the mattress and repeated her practice of grabbing the girl by the hair on the back of her head and forcing her face into the mattress and rubbing it against the mattress."

Lou Chaney was a technician assigned to the Hospital Cottage. She had been trained at the Colorado Psychopathic Hospital and hired as a Resident Supervisor. Mrs. Chaney also told of an experience with Debby Carson in the Rose Room. It made Jean Reeb's tale seem mild.

While I was working at Hospital Cottage, Debby Carson
was confined in it. She was seventeen years old and had
emotional problems involving her home life. It was some-
time during the summer that Debby had an emotional
upset and became belligerent. Mrs. Culpepper instructed
that she was to be confined in the Rose Room of Hospital
Cottage and directed that a maintenance man, Mr. Terpin,
was to help put her in the room. Mrs. Culpepper and a
nurse were present. They removed all her clothes while
Mr. Terpin was present. Debby, who was completely
naked, called Mr. Terpin a 'bastard,' among other things,
and he swung at her with his fist, striking her on the left
breast. Mrs. Culpepper was present then and ordered
Debby handcuffed behind her back and her feet were
tied to the handcuffs—she was lying on her stomach. Also
at Mrs. Culpepper's direction she was given a hypo to
calm her down. Debby was screaming, and Mrs. Culpepper grabbed her by the hair and rubbed her face *very*
forcibly in the mattress and screamed at her to be quiet.
Debby stayed in this position for four or five hours, and
was confined to the Rose Room for a number of days.

When the Rose Room offered no hope for breaking defiant
girls, staff people said that Miss Portner and Mrs. Culpepper
encouraged their escape from the school. In one case, anyway,
the kid just wasn't buying.

Flora Nieves was a resident of Mount View, but was sent,
because of her conduct, to the Colorado Psychopathic Hospital
in Pueblo. She stayed at the hospital for a long time, but
she improved and was sent back to the school. Immediately on
her return she was confined to the Rose Room. Both her
hands and feet were handcuffed to the bed in the room. She
lay, hands and feet handcuffed to the bed, for two days.

It was then, according to testimony, that Mrs. Culpepper
tried to get one of the staff people to get Flora to escape. This
staff member was to bring Flora's clothes to the Rose Room,

tell her that she felt badly about her being locked in that solitary cell, and help her escape. The staff member did not do what she was asked.

A few days later, Mrs. Culpepper allowed Flora to be released from the Rose Room and left orders that she be permitted to attend school. The expressed purpose of this turnabout was to make it convenient for Flora to run away. But Flora did not run away.

Consequently, it was arranged that Flora would be allowed to make home visits for five or six days at a stretch. Again, the assumption was that she would not return to the school when the home visit period was up. But she did.

Flora is now paroled from the school.

After all of this, ponder a while a few points of Colorado Criminal Law:

Section 40–7–22

If the warden of the penitentiary or any servant, officer or agent belonging to or in the employment of the same, or any sheriff, deputy sheriff or jailer, or any other person employed by them as a guard, shall fraudulently contrive, procure, aid, connive at, or otherwise voluntarily suffer the escape of any person in custody, every such person on conviction shall be punished by confinement in said penitentiary for a term not less than one year or more than ten years.

Section 40–7–10

Every jailer who shall be guilty of wilful inhumanity or oppression to any prisoner under his care or custody shall be fined in any sum not exceeding five hundred dollars and removed from office.

Section 40–13–1

It shall be unlawful for any person having the care or custody of any child, wilfully to cause or permit the life of such child to be endangered or the health of such child to be injured or wilfully to cause or permit such a child to be placed in such a situation that its life or health may be endangered, or wilfully or unnecessarily to be exposed to the inclemency of the weather, or to abandon such child, or to torture, torment, cruelly punish or wilfully and negligently deprive of necessary food, clothing, or shelter or in any other manner injure such child.

A little piece of the law, but it points out a big truth: that laws are only as effective as their use. Almost all states have an abundance of laws that were written to protect children from physical and psychological tormenting at the hands of their keepers. Almost all states have laws that were written to protect children from the misuse of institutional power. But these laws do not prevent anything unless they represent at least a potential threat to people who may be, for whatever reason, motivated to break them. And in Colorado, for Betty Portner and Mary Lou Culpepper, the law was no threat at all.

It came down to this. In apparent violation of almost every guideline for the care and treatment of children, in apparent violation of the legal rights of all of them, and apparently in violation of specific criminal, civil, and federal statutes, two old women were in control of the lives and destiny of hundreds of young women, and no one who cared could stop them. Why didn't state officials act? Did they have access to the allegations of wrongdoing at Mount View? And what about the public? Did it know? Did it care? Could it really do anything? It would be a while before I understood the mechanism of immunity.

Everything I have reported here, and more, much more, was forwarded by the Colorado Civil Service Employees Association lawyer, John Barnard, now a judge in Boulder, to the top officials of the state government. Copies went to Governor John Love, to David Hammil, head of the Department of Institutions, to the State Attorney General, and to others, in November, 1968, when the statements were received. There was no response.

About that same time, wonderfully pro-kid and progressive Denver Juvenile Court judge, Ted Rubin, was trying to come to grips with what he knew to be the case at Mount View. After doing what he could to verify the information that came to him through his court about the conditions at Mount View, and finding little support for change anywhere in the state government, Judge Rubin declared that he could not, in good conscience, send girls there, unless he had no alternative. Since Rubin's courtroom was not the only source of supply of girls for the school, and since the other Juvenile Court judge in Denver did not cooperate, Judge Rubin's pronouncement was seen as more symbolic than anything else by the disconnected forces who opposed the Portner-Culpepper rule. For the girls who didn't get sent there, however, Judge Rubin's courageous act was more inspired than symbolic.

He continued working to reform the Penal Code as it related to kids, developed a model halfway house to show as an alternative to institutions like Mount View, and in general served as a model of an enlightened judge. In 1970, directly related to his well-earned reputation as a champion and advocate for kids who need help, Ted Rubin was defeated for re-election by the people of Denver.

In the late sixties, Ted Rubin was one of a few public officials to challenge the destructiveness of Mount View, while elected officials who had both the power and the responsibility to make the needed changes in personnel and program at

Mount View played it safe and did nothing. Betty Portner had accumulated a lot of contacts in the state system during her thirty-five-year tour of duty and no one seemed the least bit willing to tangle publicly with her, even with all of the evidence available. Again, the enigmatic power of the entrenched was more than a match for justice.

Only a few understood the power that the Portner-Culpepper axis had over the State of Colorado and even the usual power of the press was helpless to combat it.

Within the state system, two men were working to diminish Betty Portner's power, Mylton Kennedy, the Director of the Division of Youth Services, and his Assistant at that time, Goodrich Walton. These two and Ted Rubin shared the total effective opposition to Portner rule, and even they questioned how effective they really were. Every time any one of them made a pronouncement to Portner's displeasure, they were threatened and pressured from above. Every time they would try to block or diminish what they considered a destructive policy or action of Portner's, even though they had the legal and institutional power to do so, they would find their own power strangely diminished. When Betty Portner wanted them neutralized, they were neutralized.

For twenty-five years, Betty Portner had it all her own way. As long as there was no outside "interference," Portner's rule had been absolute. But around 1960, professional staff was added to Mount View, thus letting psychiatrists, chaplains, and others—people who were not intimidated by the loss of the two or three hundred dollars a month that nonprofessional staff had to survive on—have some sort of first-hand view of the operation. With twenty-five years of total control, with buildings built by her and named for her, Portner wasn't about to give up her dictatorship without a fight. And so she fought.

Through the sixties she met her opposition, both internal

and external, with the self-assurance of royalty. Whatever small inconvenience periodic exposés and investigations may have caused, they were absorbed and forgotten. Only the investigators and the instigators felt any long-term effects. But Mylton Kennedy, Goodrich Walton and Ted Rubin did not back off. They were just forced to go slow.

A number of those connected with Mount View and Youth Services believed that Betty Portner's source of power was the wife of the governor. Portner, they felt, had the ear of the governor's wife, who in turn had the ear of the governor. And usually that meant the end of that. If the attack came from inside the state government it was easy, with the governor on her side, to shut it off. If it came from outside, forces within the government could be mobilized to give support to Portner or to simply ignore the pressure. Miss Portner also had an ace in the hole; she had spent years cultivating the club women of Colorado, and they, too, were available as a standing lobby should she need protection. The ladies were impressed by Miss Portner's frequent talks before them, where she spoke of "her girls" and the evil, immoral hell they were being saved from at Mount View. She represented righteousness, morality, and purification. She entertained them often with Mount View's Choir, the one extracurricular activity allowed the girls at the school, and the club ladies were impressed with what they saw and heard. It is doubtful that any of them ever saw Mrs. Culpepper at work in the Rose Room. And, as a matter of fact, most—but not all—of the people who suspected that Portner had an ally in the governor's wife were certain that she, too, had been fooled by Portner's other face.

Despite her formidable array of allies, however, Miss Portner's rule was, by the end of the 1960s, under almost continual challenge from within and without. Early in 1970, State Senator Anthony Vollack issued a public call for a state investigation into goings-on at Mount View, based on the statements quoted earlier in this chapter. When the story broke in the papers, Betty Portner flatly denied the charges, and blamed them on a "malicious" employee—Jean Reeb—who had been fired and who was appealing her dismissal to the Civil Service Commission. Father Knapp's allegations were dismissed by Miss Portner as "ridiculous." According to Portner, Knapp quit the priesthood to marry and "was not suited to the priesthood. . . . He was . . . well, I won't say." The allegations against Mrs. Culpepper's treatment of girls in the Rose Room met similar strong denials from Miss Portner: no one had been confined to the Rose Room for more than a month; no one's face had been smashed into the mattress; and "there is no physical abuse that I am aware of."

Mylton Kennedy and Goodrich Walton kept the pressure on, cutting back Portner's rule a little at a time. Ted Rubin worked for more community-based alternatives to Mount View and to Golden, the equally destructive Colorado boys' school, and continued his work in the juvenile justice field even after his defeat in 1970. He is still working in it. I hope the citizens of Denver discover how rare and important a man like Rubin is and convince him to return to elective office before too many more kids get ground up in the legal system.

By the summer of 1971, Betty Portner's total rule had been sufficiently chopped down by her "superiors" at Youth Services, and life wasn't the same old easy play anymore. There were a lot of people looking over her shoulder, including the psychiatric team toward which she had expressed such animosity when I had visited, and new programs instituted by Walton opened the school enough to let some light shine in.

In June, 1971, Betty Portner "retired." She received the best wishes and congratulations of the governor's wife and the club ladies, and a special commendation from President Nixon. She immediately launched herself as a speaker on "law and order." A month later, Mary Lou Culpepper was bumped through a rather complicated issue of seniority and was left without an institution. Goodrich Walton temporarily assumed the Directorship at Mount View, and the Portner era suddenly and quietly ended.

I spoke with Walton after he had handed the institution over to an acting director to carry out the much-needed reforms of Mount View and had reassumed his position of Director of Youth Services. I was most interested in learning how the Portner era had gone on for as long as it did and how, if at all, another one could be prevented in Denver or anywhere.

He began cautiously. "We don't really know if Betty Portner's approach and attitude was effective because we don't have any valid research. What we had here was an absolute authoritarian, moralistic, self-righteous attitude about 'little ladies' and what they should and shouldn't do, and there was no measurement about what would happen to them if you subjected them to this kind of a thing. The fact of the matter is that a lot of girls that came to the girls' school were in such bad trouble because they didn't sleep, didn't eat properly, they were subjected to all kinds of problems; so that when they came to the girls' school they got a lot healthier, they grew a little older, and when they got out of there, maybe they were a little more capable, in spite of what Betty did to them, to cope."

It seemed to be a high price to pay for adding some health and some years. "Isn't there something better than that to offer kids?" I asked. "Something better than letting them get older? How did Betty Portner get by with giving them so little?"

"Well," Walton answered, "this rigid, authoritarian thing and this self-righteous, moralistic attitude—most of the people here subscribe to it, most of the people in any state subscribe to it, and they don't give a damn whether it works or not."

Walton went on: "The worst thing you could do to try to get people to live in communities is to put them in institutions. I do not believe in institutionalization for most of the people that have been sent to the girls' school or to the boys' school in the last fifty or a hundred years. I am very much in favor of trying to deal with them in the community and trying to deal with their parents and their environments in such a way that they are better able to make it. I think that when you separate them from where they're going to live that you don't do much in the way of reintegration at all. This old rehabilitation concept doesn't make a hell of a lot of sense when it's put into an institutional setting that's totally artificial."

Then he said what others around the country had told me, but he said it with a special clarity and fervor. I had asked him about the kids who just couldn't make it in the community. The kids who are always thrown up to institutional reformers as the reasons the institutions are necessary.

"My opinion is that probably 60 percent of the girls ever sent to the Girls' School and 50 percent of the boys ever sent to the Boys' School should have never been sent there in the last fifty years; that the treatment program does nothing for them—it's a wrong thing—it does them more harm than good.

"In the best of worlds, we would receive and evaluate kids in trouble and try either to reintegrate them in the community if the diagnosis or prognosis is in that direction. But if they are really, in fact, threats to the welfare of other people in the community, if they're assaultive or if they've got character disorders, we do really need to have some kind of institution.

"But the institution is an aberration unless it is geared to their needs."

I asked Walton how, in the face of public opinion, the Betty Portners of the child-care establishment can be replaced by sensitive and creative people. "Do we," I asked, "have to wait until these people die off?"

"Yes. Because in state service you can't fire them. There is no way you can fire a Portner. She wouldn't even be criticized, because of the women's groups in the state who loved her and have a lot of political muscle. And when it seems that you've got her getting to the governor's wife, there's no way you can intercede in this situation. So it has to be by attrition. If they get old enough so that they die off or have to retire as she did, you have some hope.

"But we're in a situation where terribly neurotic compulsive bookkeepers are running the whole damn state. There aren't any people in the General Assembly who are basically concerned about kids and with this kind of a legislature and the public so willing to leave things the way they are, we just simply don't know what the hell's going to happen and it's not a rosy picture at all."

Goodrich Walton is a good man, one who would have made kids much better off if he had been allowed to give himself totally to his job unobstructed by the political power of "neurotic compulsive bookkeepers," women's clubs, and governors' wives. One wonders what such a man could have done if he had had the freedom to act for the kids who were sent needlessly into "treatment" at Mount View. And one wonders how many would never have gone there at all.

Soon after he finds "the right man" to be permanent director of Mount View, Goodrich Walton will retire. He has faith that the "young people that are coming on are good" and that "they can and probably will change the system." In the meantime, there are living children to consider.

In Denver, you can begin with the boys' school.

3

Louisiana

The Hole
and the
Hosepipe

Kids sent to Scotlandville, the State Industrial School for
Youth near Baton Rouge, Louisiana, came back telling the
same stories of beatings and other mistreatment with such
regularity that the stories lost their shock—people just nodded
the long-suffering understanding of the poor and tried as best
they could to keep their kids out of there. As usual, many were
unsuccessful and their kids were processed through a careless
legal system into the brutalization they called "Reform" school.
Four such kids speak here. They were sixteen and seventeen
when I met with them in a community center in New Orleans.
Each of them spent his early teens in confinement at Scotlandville.

Notice particularly how and why they got there, the matter-
of-fact way they discuss their experiences, and, maybe most
important of all, the sense of justice that remains in them
along with an unexplainable belief in the good intentions of

authority. It remains an incredible fact that kids place so little blame for their pains on the society that inflicts them; they want so much to believe that the adult world is worth growing into, even more to believe that adults somehow "really" care. For this wish, kids are willing to stretch reality.

My name is Richard and I was in the Maplewood Cottage. Mr. John Smitty beat us with hosepipe, beat us with these big sticks—sticks come off a tree—and like our mommas would send us something in the mail, he takes it up to his apartment and keeps it for himself. Momma sends you a carton of cigarettes, he don't give you no more'n fo' packs, keeps six. He beat us with his fist, anythin' when he gets mad.

Q. What does he get mad at?

A. When him and his wife get in an argument, he take it out on the boys.

Q. How many boys were there in your cottage?

A. About ninety somethin' in our cottage.

Q. Was there enough room for that many guys?

A. Yeah. Enough room. They had some sleepin on the flo', y' know, slept on the flo' with a spread.

Q. Do you remember the first day you were there? What was it like?

A. They didn't tell me nothin', they just tighten me up and put me on the dormitory—give me my clothes, y' know. They didn't tell me how the rules and regulations was or nothin'. You can't talk, y' know, when you're sittin' around the TV room, y' can't talk to your friends—the only time they treat you nice is on visitin' Sunday when your parents come, then they treat you like you're s'posed to be treated.

Q. You ever go to school? Was there any school?

A. There was school, but they don't learn you nothin'. You sit in school all day and play cards. That's all. They don't give you no books, nothin' like that. They don't teach us nothin'.

And the teachers just set around and talk with other teachers, that's all.

Q. What about food? What was a typical meal like?

A. They give you hash, sometimes they give you cheese instead, two slices of bread, and a little thing of somethin' t' drink.

Q. Did you ever have a medical examination? Medical care? Dental?

A. They didn't give you none of that—none of that.

Q. How long did you spend there?

A. I stood there a year and eight months. I didn't know what happened, how long I would be there, nothin' till the day I was t' leave.

Q. Did you ever spend any time in "the hole"?

A. The hole? Yeah. I spent two weeks there.

Q. What is the hole all about? How did you get in there?

A. I was in school and I was talkin' to this little girl. Y' see, they don't want you talkin' to the girls. The little girl, y' know, was a close friend of mine, she know my daddy and my daddy been knowin' her since she was a baby. Me and her was talkin' and she gave me three cigarettes. The man saw me and knocked me down. Then he gave her a couple of days in the hole and put me in the boys' side.

Q. What was the hole like?

A. The hole, it's like, don't have no beds or nothin' where you sit. There's one toilet in it, you sit down in there—its a little cell, y' know, with one toilet.

Q. How many guys are there in that one cell?

A. Ten, fifteen, in one cell. Nowhere to sleep, sit up all night. You go in there with your underwears on, undershirt, you're black and dirty when you come out.

Q. How long did you stay there?

A. I stood there two weeks. Some of them stay thirty days,

two months. They don't feed you but a little piece of corn bread and a little round piece of grits, that's all; you ask for some water, they don't give you no water, y' know. If they *do* give you any water it'd be hot water from the faucet. They give it to you in a little plastic cup, just a cup of water if they want to. Very seldom y' get water.

Q. Is there any light or air in the hole?

A. There's no kind of air. They got windows but they keep them closed. Cages over 'em. Iron bars, y' know. They keep the windows locked and covered up.

Q. Is there any light?

A. No, sir. There ain't no electricity in the hole. No light at all 'cept when they open the door.

Q. Did anybody get real sick while you were there?

A. A lot of 'em got sick. Rushed 'em all to Zachery Hospital —when you tell 'em you're sick they're not gonna believe you until the last minute. They'd rather see you sufferin', y' know?

Q. Did very many guys try to run away, to escape?

A. Yeah. Most of 'em tried to run away because of that reason, because they don't treat 'em nice.

Q. What happens when they catch them?

A. If they catch 'em, they beat 'em and bring 'em back, then they lock 'em down in the hole for two or three months.

Q. Did you ever get beaten up yourself?

A. I got beat up twice. My housefather beat me with a stick.

Q. What was his name?

A. John Smith. John Smitty, of the Maplewood Cottage.

Q. How bad were you hurt?

A. See where he cut me on my eye? I got a cut on my left eye where he knocked me out.

Q. What were you doing?

A. We were all watchin' TV and I got up to ask him can I use the bathroom and he started punchin' me all over my face and then he knocked me out and kicked me in my side. I tried hittin' him back but I got knocked out. Then after that he was hatin' me as long as I was in there. Then another time he jumped on me after visitin' Sunday. He didn't like the way I was walkin', y' know, went to beatin' on me. I didn't raise my hands on him that time because I was makin' seventeen and I didn't want to be sent to prison.

Q. Do you mind if I ask you what the charge was that they sent you up there for?

A. They had me for sniffing glue.

Q. That was it?

A. That was all.

Q. And you were there for a year and—

A. A year and eight months. Went there when I was fifteen, till my seventeenth birthday.

Q. Did they ever have any visitors from the state government?

A. Judges come up there, y' know, when we'd be in school. And when they'd be walkin' around, they wouldn't let nobody talk to 'em, y' see? Somebody go to talk to 'em, they'd make 'em go back. A whole lot of boys been breakin' out, tryin' to tell somebody, y' know, wishin' that somebody come up there and they could talk to 'em how it is, y' know, but they wouldn't let nobody get a chance to talk with 'em. If one of us try to go up and talk to 'em and try to tell somethin', they bring us back and put us in the hole. They don't want us to tell what's goin' on. If whoever came to visit would say, "don't lock 'em up," they probably don't do it until after they leave. They'd still end up beatin' 'em. They beat you bad up there, that's the truth.

Q. Was your "housefather" the worst?

A. Yeah, he was one of the worst, but they got lots more. They don't like New Orleans boys at all.

Q. Did any kids die while you were up there?

A. Naw, nobody died while I was up there. They got beat to death though.

Q. That's what I'm talking about. I don't mean die of old age. Was there anyone in the whole place you could go to to help you out?

A. Only person could help you out was the Superintendent and they wouldn't let us get to him.

Q. What kind of guy is he?

A. He own the whole campus.

Q. Is he a good guy or a bad guy?

A. Yeah, he's a good guy. But he don't know what's goin' on, y' see? He don't *be's* on the dormitory. Very seldom he go back to the dormitories.

Q. Do you think that he really doesn't know that all this stuff is going on?

A. *He don't know.* He *definitely* don't know. One time we had run out of the dormitory and told him about it. He didn't know. They had a couple of men fired for beatin' a boy, bustin' his backside. He fired a couple of 'em. A boy went and told how he was bleedin' bad, y' know. But he definitely don't know everything that's goin' on in there.

Q. What's an average day like? Tell me what you do from when you wake up.

A. Well, you wake up at five in the morning—quarter to five—come downstairs, half of us go to the bathroom, brush our teeth, then the other half goes. Then we sit down and watch TV. We don't eat till eight o'clock. Then school from eight-thirty to eleven-thirty, then we go eat. From one o'clock to four o'clock we stay in school. Then maybe watch a little TV. Summertime they make you get out in the sun and march like you're in the army or somethin'.

Q. There are girls in the same school, right?

A. Yeah, in the same school but they put them in different classes.

Q. Do you have any contact at all with them? Socials? Dances? Anything at all?

A. Maybe on the last day of school the girls' cottage would have a dance but everybody can't go.

Q. How did they finally decide to let you go?

A. They just sent my discharge papers.

Q. Then you could have been there two weeks or two years or ten? You didn't know?

A. I coulda been up there longer, till the judge decide I could come home and 'lessen they write and tell him that I was doin' all right, I'd still be there.

Q. This might be a hard question to answer, but what do you think you learned up there at Scotlandville?

A. The only thing I learned was how to play cards good at school and how to make checkerboards. That's all I learned.

My name is Matthew. I want to add somethin'. When I first went up there they didn't tell me nothin'. They just tighten me up and put me in a dormitory, and I didn't know how that you're not supposed to go in the back and use the bathroom on your own. I got up and was walkin' in the back to use the bathroom and the man picked up the can that you put your cigarettes in and hit me in the head with it.

Q. Who was the man?

A. Mr. Claiborne.

Q. Is he still up there?

A. Yeah, he's still there.

Q. What's the thing about going to the bathroom?

A. You have to ask permission and sometimes they tell you no and you have to just wet on yourself or do what you gotta do on yourself. They let you go if they want to let you go.

Q. How long were you up there?

A. Eleven months and three weeks.

Q. Did you ever talk to anyone while you were there to find out how long you were going to stay?

A. I went to see my counselor after I was there six months and I had to sneak to see him. I was working in the dining hall and I snuck over there. He told me I was goin' home next month and I stood up there eleven months and three weeks.

Q. During that eleven months and three weeks, how many times did you see that counselor?

A. One time. That first time when I snuck over there.

Q. Is that how it is with most of the guys? They don't see a counselor any more than that?

A. Yes, sir, 'less a counselor knows his parents or somethin', then he might call you over every week and talk to you.

Q. Did you ever get knocked around except for that first day when you learned about the bathroom?

A. Yes, sir. One time they were only 'sposed to take nine to the dinin' hall and I was number ten in line and the house-father, he just pulled me out of line and hit me with a hose-pipe. Then I just had to stay and wait while everyone else went to eat.

Q. Where do they get these hosepipes so fast? Do they always carry them around with them?

A. Yes, sir, in their back pockets. They have them balled up so that nobody can see them like when the Superintendent walks in—and he never said he was sorry or nothin'—even when the man told him that I worked in the dinin' hall and I was 'sposed to go. He never even said he was sorry.

Q. Did you go to school while you were there?

A. I went to school the first two months.

Q. What was it like?

A. All you do is go in the classroom, sit down at a table, they might have five around the table or eight, sometimes ten, squeezed around one table, and there'd be a deck of cards for the table or a checkerboard or somethin'.

Q. And that's school?

A. Yes, sir.

Q. Did you get any medical attention at all? Any physical examinations?

A. No. When I first worked in the dining hall they took a stool specimen, that's all.

Q. Who were the worst guys there as far as you remember?

A. Mr. Span and Mr. Claiborne.

Q. What about Mr. Span?

A. He hits you with a stick, an oak stick, that he cuts three little notches in, and every time he hit you he puts three little notches in your backside. One time he was real mad with the boys in the dormitory and he hit every boy with that stick, bust their backsides. Five of the boys had nerve enough to sneak to the Superintendent and tell him and he got sent off for a month about that.

Q. Was there anything good about the place?

A. Only thing good about it was when the Superintendent be talkin' to us in chapel. That's the only thing.

Q. If you could change it, if you could make it over, what would you do?

A. I'd let everybody have the same rights. I'd treat all of 'em the same. I wouldn't let one have special things and not let everyone else have them. And I wouldn't beat 'em like no dogs. I'd have punishments if you do something wrong, take privileges away or take your smoking from you. They don't do that. They'd rather beat you.

Q. What was the youngest kid there that you remember?

A. Six years old.

Q. Were there many that young?

A. No, there was one six, but there was a lot of others seven and eight.

Q. What was the six-year-old there for?

A. He was with his brother when his brother stole a car. His brother was older than him. His brother was fourteen and he was six years old. So they convicted both of 'em.

Q. How long did the six-year-old stay there?

A. Seven or eight months. Him and his brother stayed the same time and they went on together.

Q. Did he stay in the same dormitory as his older brother?

A. At first they had him in the little dormitory with the little boys but he used to cry every day and every night. He wanted to be where his brother was. He was losin' weight and everything and got sick. One of the men up there was his cousin so he fixed it up so he could be with his brother.

Q. How old were the little guys in the little dormitory?

A. About six to nine or ten.

Q. Were there many that age?

A. Yeah.

Q. What were they there for?

A. Maybe they'd be with someone who did somethin' and they'd just send both of 'em up.

Q. Were they treated the same as the older kids, the way you described?

A. They had one man up there that'd treat 'em right, their regular housefather, but he only worked four days, the other days they had another man come on, Mr. Simms, and he used to hit those little boys up the side of the head, knock the little boys down and hit 'em with a hosepipe. He had a special little skinny hosepipe, a skinny green hosepipe for them.

Q. He had a little hosepipe for the little kids, huh?

A. A little skinny hosepipe. For the big boys he had a big fat hosepipe. He'd make little boys put their hands on the wall and tell 'em "don't move," but hittin' 'em it would hurt, naturally they would move their hands and try to rub or somethin'.

Q. Did they ever send any little kids to the hole?

A. Yes, sir.

Q. What was the youngest kid you ever saw in there?

A. Seven years old. And he was banged up for sneakin' to the dining hall. He was hungry and wanted something to eat. They put him in school and he snuck from school and went to the dining hall and they caught him comin' back with some corn bread—he was eatin' it walkin' back towards the school and they caught him and put him in the hole. He stood down there for three weeks. They put him in a cell with those big boys 'stead of puttin' him in a cell by hisself or with some little boys. They put him in a cell with boys fifteen, sixteen, and fourteen years old and here he was nothin' but seven years old. Some of them was takin' the little boy's food and stuff and beatin' him all up. And if he hollered for the man, the man would come back and tell him that's good for him.

My name's Martin.

Q. How did you get in there?

A. Glue.

Q. How long did you spend there?

A. Eight months a week and four days.

Q. What kind of trial did you have?

A. It lasted a few minutes. Judge took a look at me, pluck his cigar and told me to get on out of there. Man took me to Youth Study Center, then took me to Scotlandville.

Q. How many times have you been in front of the same judge? You been in front of him before?

A. That was my first time ever in court.

Q. Glue-sniffing was the first time you were ever in court and you got sent up for . . . how long was that?

A. Eight months a week and four days. And for eight months a week and four days I ain't learnt nothin' up there.

Q. Can you think of any reason that a place like Scotland-ville ought to be there?

A. If it changed it'd be a reason.

Q. Do you think there's some kids that need to be away from home?

A. Yes, sir, if they commit a crime after the first time where you deserve another chance. But if you make the same mistake twice, you deserve to be sent away for a little while. But I wouldn't say for as long as they been keepin' some of them boys up there.

Q. What's the longest you've ever heard a boy being there?

A. Five years. They even got bugs all in the bed. You'd be goin' to bed and the bugs would be gettin' all over you. Sometimes the springs would be all eaten up and the only way you'd get a mattress is to fight for it. Sometimes the only way you would get a bed at all was to fight for it.

Q. Was there any kind of privacy at all? Was there any place you could put your own stuff and keep it?

A. No place I could say was private.

Q. No place you could lock up something that was your own?

A. You couldn't lock it up. There'd be a locker but you couldn't lock it or nothin'. One boy snuck a lock on his locker and the housefather found out that that was his locker and called him in the back and beat him all the while until he opened it and took the lock off and gave it to him. He was down there tryin' to open it and he was steady beatin' him with a hosepipe.

Q. If I was going to go up there and visit the place tonight and they knew that I was coming up, would they come around telling everyone that there was going to be a visitor?

A. They wouldn't tell *us* nothin'. See, they send a little boy around with a note tellin' all the housefathers and the teachers, and they take their sticks and stuff and go put them in their cars—their belts and hosepipes they take and put them in their cars. And when they leave, the front office send a little boy around with a note sayin' they left, and they go get their hosepipes and stuff outta the car.

Q. So now we know where to look for the hoses. You wanted to say something else.

A. Yeah. In the winter they'd have you go out there with no gloves on, housefathere'd be havin' you wash his car. They'd pick a boy out, y' know, like, "you, you, and you go out there and wash my car," and when you come back and it's not done right, they'd send you out there again and tell you the next time you come back it better be done right. You don't have no choice because if you don't do it right the second time, you come back and you know he's gonna beat you. And they wouldn't even tell you "thank you" or nothin', or buy you a pack of cigarettes for washin' their cars.

My name is St. George and I was convicted for sniffing glue. I stayed up there for a year and one month. Mr. Span gave me forty licks with a stick, busted my head and my backside.

Q. Were beatings a regular thing? Did somebody get beaten up every day or once a week or what?

A. All the time. Every night somebody catchin' a beatin'. They don't have no limit to licks. One time they gave a boy a hundred licks for smokin' in the TV room. He was supposed to be givin' me seven licks but he was pullin' a lie. Every time he beat the boys, they rub, y' know? And jump around. So I stood up there and go across the chair. I took my seven licks straight. He got mad, y' know. He called me back. He was mad because I didn't rub. I took 'em straight. So he *broke* that stick on me. He went across and got a stick from another dormitory and gave me forty licks, bust my backside.

They got a lot of kids up there for not going to school. They send you up there for not going to school and you still don't learn nothin' *up there*. That don't make you change that you want to go to school.

Q. How long did guys spend up there for not going to school?

A. One stood three years for not goin' to school. One boy's been up there six years. Been there since he was nine years old, 'cause his momma died. He had a charge of stealin' some four dollars out of a little girl's wallet before his momma died. When his momma died they sent him to Scotlandville. His brother tried to help him out and got in an argument with his probation officer—the probation officer sent *him* up with him. Both stood up there, one stood five years, the other six years 'cause he committed the crime.

Q. You mean he's been up there six years for a four-dollar crime?

A. Yes, sir. Even I didn't believe it at first, but I asked his counselor.

Q. Did they use pills? Did they give the guys pills, tranquilizers, or any kind of pills regularly?

A. Medicine?

Q. Well, yeah, medicine.

A. Some of 'em were put on pills. Pills that make you sleepy, dizzy, and like that.

Q. Do you know a lot of guys that they kept on those pills?

A. Yeah. I was on 'em. I got on 'em because my parole officer asked me, did I love my mother? And I said, "Yeah, I love my mother." He ask me, will I *kill* my mother? I say no! I ask him, "Would you kill yours?" Y' know? He said, I need to be treated. They put me on fifty milligrams, little pills that made me sleep all day.

Q. What did the pills look like?

A. Little round blue pills. They just told me, "You better take 'em," that's all.

Q. How often did they make you take them?

A. Every evening and eight o'clock in the morning.

Q. Wasn't the reason that you were in there for sniffing glue?

A. Yeah.

Q. Then they end up giving you pills?

A. Yeah.

Q. Kind of interesting logic. Would you say that more than half or less than half was taking some kind of medicine that made them drowsy?

A. More than half. Mostly all of 'em was taking some kind of medicine. They make you work in the fields and when you can't work they give you *methadrine*. One guy it made him dizzy for eight months. But most of 'em was on some kind of pills. Either the blue ones or the red ones. Forty-two out of our dormitory was taking pills at eight in the morning and at night before they go to bed about six o'clock.

Q. Were all the drugs given by a doctor?

A. The nurses.

Q. Were any of you checked by a doctor? Did the doctor order the medicine or did the nurse order the medicine?

A. I don't know.

Q. Did you *ever* go to the doctor when you were at Scotlandville?

A. No, sir.

Q. You never saw a doctor?

A. Not me, no. Never.

Q. Then who was the one who made the decision to give you the medicine?

A. The nurse.

Q. You don't know who decided that some guys should get medicine and some guys shouldn't?

A. I just know that one morning they come over with my name to take medicine. I don't know nothin' about no doctor tellin' me he was goin' to put me on somethin'. I didn't see no doctor. And nobody told me he was gonna put me on medicine.

Y' see the dormitory I was in was spozed to be for people kind of off.

Q. Did you have a special counselor or housefather?

A. Yeah. I was in Magnolia. Mr. Aaronson was my housefather.

Q. What was he like?

A. He kinda off too.

Q. When the three of you got arrested, what happened? Were you taken to a juvenile hall or what? What happened before you got to Scotlandville?

A. They take you to Youth Study Center.

Q. What happens there?

A. You're locked up in a room with a piece of concrete with a little mattress on it. Twenty-four hours a day you be in a room all by yourself and all you hear is keys jingling—keys jingling and big old doors slamming.

Q. How long did it take you until you had a hearing?

A. A month.

A. A month three weeks and four days.

A. Three months.

Q. You stayed there three months before you had a trial?

A. Yes, sir.

Q. How much can you speak in your own defense?

A. Nothin'. Y' see, you bring me in or you got the charge on me, the judge is gonna ask you what happened. My word don't mean nothin'. If you say I done it, I done it. I'll get time.

Q. Regardless of what you say?

A. Regardless. I can't say nothin'.

Q. Did you have a lawyer?

A. Nobody has one in Juvenile Court. You just have a probation officer.

Q. No lawyer? Do they still not have lawyers in juvenile cases?

A. No, just a probation officer. That's why so many of 'em get sent away.

Q. Can the parents say anything at the time of the trial?

A. Well, they did ask my mom did she ever hear of me gettin' in trouble around the neighborhood and she said, "No, but I don't be round him all the time, he might be gettin' into some kind of trouble." Y' know parents, they wouldn't take up for no son or nothin', y' know. If the court think they're wrong, they're wrong. They wouldn't try to talk 'em into not sendin' you away to reform school, y' know.

Q. What would happen if the mother said you never got in any trouble and never had any complaints from neighbors? What would happen in a case like that? Would it have any effect?

A. It still wouldn't do no good, but I never heard anyone's momma say nothin' like that. It's usually like when I walk in court. I just walk in court and in a few minutes the judge read the sentence. I say, "Can I say somethin'?" He say, "Nope—State Industrial School." He don't wanna hear nothin'.

Q. Who sets the amount of time?

A. The judge. He gives you an indefinite period. That's from six months to a year, a year and six months to two years—this could go on and on, to five or six years, whenever they get ready.

Q. Let me understand this now. Of all you guys, none of you ever had a lawyer in court. Is that right?

A. Yes.

A. Yeah.

A. Yes.

Q. Do you think the judge that sent you up there, and I want you to answer this individually, do you think the judge thought the place was the way it was or do you think that he didn't know?

A. He didn't know.

A. They don't know

A. He don't know. They come up there—like a judge would come to visit—they'd try to clean the place up, straighten it up. They even give you a good meal then. Then after they leave, everything would change back to the way it was.

Q. Do you think that the judge thought that by you going up there you'd come back better off?

A. Yes, sir.

STATE INDUSTRIAL SCHOOL
FOR COLORED YOUTH
BATON ROUGE 7, LOUISIANA

Reaching for freedom

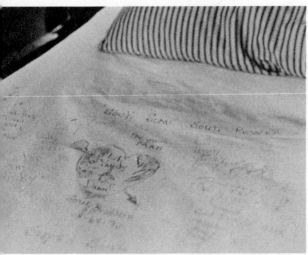

Graffiti on the sheets
at Scotlandville

The classroom at Scotlandville

Barbed wire

Backless chairs at Scotlandville

Occupational therapy:
washing a counselor's car

The distaff side of Scotlandville

Lunch for
visitors to see

Looking through
the bars at
Scotlandville

Sleeping on the floor at Scotlandville

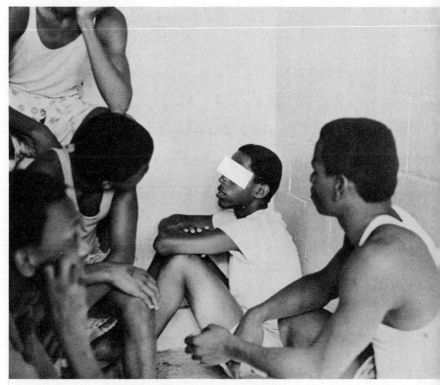

In the hole at Scotlandville

Scotlandville's library

Dormitory windows

Recreation

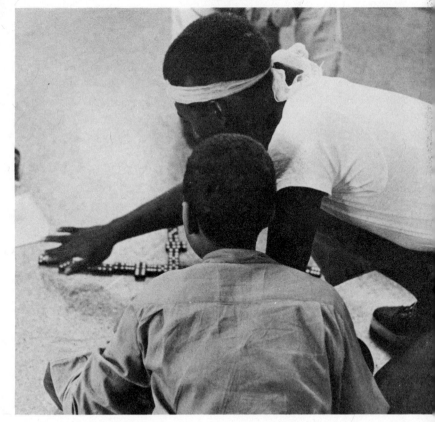

Zen basketball

The Distaff Side of Scotlandville: Malice in Wonderland

Life at Scotlandville, as described by the young men who just told their stories, had many similarities to the world outside. The young people were oppressed by uncaring adults, the means of survival forced the early death of childhood if not the child, the rules that applied to white kids and "rich" kids did not apply to them, and there wasn't much to look forward to, or to do or care about. Like America's other kid prisons, Scotlandville was just a smaller, more intense, more confined and confining version of the broader and more permissive prisons we call ghettos. And like the ghetto outside, the one constructed by the State of Louisiana for "rehabilitation" and "training" did not discriminate when it came to their sisters. Young women shared the confinement at Scotlandville—shared the oppressive and uncaring adults and all the rest, but shared them and suffered them separately. Boys and girls were allowed to see each other but not to talk to or touch each other, except on special occasions. Strategic use of these "special occasions" was one of the most powerful means of social control available to the Scotlandville staff.

The following is a section of a Federal Court action brought in behalf of three girls imprisoned in Scotlandville for undefined "improper" behavior before a Juvenile Court judge after they had been illegally arrested for unknown charges. In its own way it speaks clearly and dramatically of the madness we call justice for children. I have changed names and addresses that might make it possible to identify the children.

The writ was filed in Federal Court because the Juvenile Court said simply that it would not honor a writ, and the Criminal Court said it did not have jurisdiction over a juvenile case. As I had found so many times, the implementation of a "good idea," in this instance the Juvenile Court system, had become a mask to hide destructive practices. While the Juvenile Court originally disregarded Constitutional guarantees in children's cases in order to give kids even greater protections, in New Orleans, as in the rest of the country, such disregard became the means of giving children practically no protection at all.

STATE OF LOUISIANA

COURT OF APPEALS FOR THE FOURTH CIRCUIT

PETITION FOR WRIT OF HABEAS CORPUS

To the Honorable Court of Appeals for the Fourth Circuit comes the petitioner, [Veronica Brown], age fifteen, pursuant to the Code of Criminal Procedure, Article 351 et seq., and respectfully represents:

I. *Statement of the Case*

1.

Petitioner is presently committed to the custody of Dallas B. Matthews, Superintendent, State Industrial School for Colored Youth, at Scotlandville, Louisiana, by order of the Honorable James P. O'Conner of the Juvenile Court of New

Orleans, Docket No. 000-000X, [date]. A copy of said order was demanded from the Clerk of Court, and refused under authority of R.S. 13:1585. Said order reads:

> [Margaret Johnson, Carol Sue Richards, and Veronica Brown] are each found delinquent and each is now committed to State Industrial School for Colored Youth with no consideration for leave or parole for two years because of behavior at Youth Study Center and courtroom.

Petitioner subsequently applied on March 11, 1969, to the Honorable Criminal District Court for the Parish of Orleans to issue the Writ of Habeas Corpus. That Honorable Court, per Judge Malcolm V. O'Hara, refused said Writ on the ground that the Criminal District Court was without jurisdiction to try, or hear an appeal from, a juvenile case, and was therefore without habeas corpus jurisdiction as well.

2.

Petitioner was arrested [date], at about 9:35 A.M., inside the home of her friend and co-defendant, [Margaret Johnson], [street], New Orleans, Louisiana. Petitioner resides at [street], New Orleans, Louisiana.

3.

On the morning of [date], petitioner was present at her friend's apartment. At approximately 8:30 A.M., Ptn. [Jones] and [O'Brien] of the New Orleans Police Department knocked at the front door of the [Johnson] apartment. [Margaret Johnson] answered the door. The officers asked whether [Carol Sue Richards] was there. She answered no. The officers then stated they wanted to search the house. She told the police they could not come inside her house without a search warrant. At this, the police officers left.

4.

Within approximately one-half hour, the same officers returned to the [Johnson] apartment, and without knocking entered the house, this time through a rear door which was not locked. [Margaret Johnson] again told the officers they could not search without a warrant. Although the officers did not have a warrant, they continued into the house.

5.

Present in the apartment besides petitioner and [Margaret Johnson] were [Carol Sue Richards] and petitioner's sister [Francine Brown], age 13. The officers asked which of the girls was [Carol Sue], and when petitioner pointed her out, they told her she would have to go down to the Juvenile Bureau. At no time did the officers announce why they were seeking out [Carol Sue Richards], nor why they were arresting her. An altercation arose, as a result of which petitioner and [Margaret Johnson], along with [Carol Sue Richards] were taken to the Juvenile Bureau at Tulane and Broad Streets, New Orleans. Petitioner was never informed that she was being arrested, nor why she was taken into custody.

6.

When petitioner arrived at the Juvenile Bureau, she asked Detective [William Allen] if she could phone her mother. He denied her request. She replied that she wanted to call her mother, because her mother worked for a lawyer who had helped her on a prior juvenile detention, but to no avail. After transfer to the Youth Study Center, 1100 Milton Street, New Orleans, petitioner was again unable to contact her parents because she understood that telephone calls were forbidden.

7.

At the Juvenile Bureau, the authorities attempted to interrogate petitioner. At no time was she informed of her right to remain silent, that anything she said could be used against her, and that she had a right to a lawyer, that if she could not afford one, one would be provided, or that if she decided to speak, she could stop at any time.

8.

Petitioner remained at the Youth Study Center until January 21, 1969, at which time she was released into the custody of her mother, [Mrs. Beverly Brown]. About two weeks later, petitioner and her mother were called to the juvenile bureau by petitioner's probation officer to discuss the case. The probation officer read a form entitled "Guarantees Afforded to Juveniles and Waiver of Guarantees," and stated that petitioner could go before the court and tell her story, or discuss it with the probation officer first. Petitioner and her mother signed the form with the understanding that the form had only to do with petitioner's right to keep silent before the probation officer. The probation officer informed them that an attorney would be appointed by the court if petitioner thought she needed one, and petitioner and her mother understood that the form they signed had nothing to do with having an attorney. Present counsel for petitioner asked to see the signed form but was refused. A blank copy is attached as Exhibit A. Neither petitioner nor her parents were informed by the court at trial that the petitioner could have counsel appointed for her or that she was entitled to same.

9.

Neither petitioner nor her parents received notice in writing of the charges against petitioner. The only official document received by petitioner's parents from the juvenile authorities was the subpoena to appear for trial, [date].

10.

Petitioner had no counsel at trial. Petitioner was not permitted to cross-examine prosecution witnesses, nor was she allowed to testify in her own behalf, nor to call witnesses in her defense. In point of fact, the Court pronounced sentence immediately after the prosecution witnesses had testified, although co-defendant [Margaret Johnson] had just previously attempted to traverse while on the stand one of the arresting officers' testimony.

11.

The length of petitioner's sentence was based in part on purported conduct in the Youth Study Center and in the courtroom, which evidence she was not permitted to controvert. In point of fact, petitioner had been incarcerated in the Youth Study Center for only four days, during which time she had conducted herself fully properly, and while in the courtroom, petitioner had remained silent for the pendency of the trial. Such evidence, relating particularly to only one of the three juvenile co-defendants, was nevertheless made the basis, indiscriminately, of the common sentence, for which the allegedly proscribed conduct was not specified, nor that it was wrong. Furthermore, such evidence was presented prior to the finding of guilty in respect of violation of the state statute (which was the basis for the delinquency decision). On information and belief, such immaterial evidence entered the guilt-finding process.

12.

Petitioner was found delinquent, R.S. 13:1570 (A) (5) by violating R.S. 14:108, relative to resisting an officer, by intentionally opposing, obstructing and acting violently towards Ptn. [Jones] and Ptn. [O'Brien], New Orleans police officers acting in their official capacity, and authorized by law, to make lawful arrest, about 9:35 A.M., January 17, 1969, at the location [street], New Orleans, Louisiana, with full knowledge that said officers were acting in their official capacity. R.S. 14:108 carries a maximum penalty of six months in jail or $300.00 fine, or both.

13.

Petitioner was sentenced to two years at the State Industrial School for Colored Youth, an all Negro institution created and maintained as such by R.S. 15:1011 et seq. Parallel institutions for white neglected and delinquent children are created by R.S. 15:911 et seq., and R.S. 15:971 et seq.

14.

Although commitment of a juvenile to said institution is declared by R.S. 15:1017 to be "not punitive nor in anywise to be construed as a penal sentence, but as a step in the total treatment process toward rehabilitation of the juvenile," said institution is not rehabilitative and is in fact merely a custodial, penal institution. Petitioner, a fifteen year old child, who was three months pregnant at the time, was for five and one-half days consigned to the "hole" or isolated confinement cell measuring nine feet by six, without shoes or a dress. The cell contained no toilet seat or toilet paper, no lights or adequate ventilation, no bed or chair, or water faucets. Meals consisted of milk, bread and a spoonful of beans, and petitioner was forced to eat with her hands because no utensils were provided. Petitioner slept on a mattress placed on the floor. Sanitary napkins for girls in the "hole" are kept uncovered in a closet in a dirty dish.

4

San Francisco

Babies
in Cages

Jean Jacobs is a San Francisco woman whose strength and compassion for kids has led her to a national award for volunteer service, a *Time* magazine feature article, and a general and persistent attraction by the public and the media puzzled by a woman in her social position devoting her life to the rights of children. In what may be her most unique attribute, Jean gracefully accepts the awards and the notice, and then pays no attention to them at all. Neither acclaim nor ridicule nor attack nor diversion has been successful in stopping Jean Jacobs from her mission: a responsible freedom for children and an end to their suffering in children's jails. She has never been a woman to settle for less than what she believes. Bureaucrats in the California kid jail system know this well.

As the founder and prime spirit behind San Francisco's Citizens for Juvenile Justice, a group Jean put together to fight the destruction of children in her city, she has helped to turn the youth institutions there in the direction of sanity. To do this, Jean has devoted herself for many years to listening to children (a generally lost art among adults), working with them and pushing hard for them in places where such pushing counts.

It wasn't always like that. Jean Jacobs didn't come to her commitment to imprisoned children in anything resembling a straight line. Only a year before the formation of the Citizens for Juvenile Justice, Jean was an active volunteer who worked within established organizations. Something happened to change all that, something that I think Jean can tell best.

As we spoke, I felt something coming through the warmth and beauty that radiate from her. It was an emotion that I had most often felt coming from the kids I knew who were trapped in the ghetto—from people who were at the bottom of this society's ladder. It was anger. And Jean was neither ghettoized nor poor. The mother of four, married to a prominent San Francisco lawyer, Jean had little of her own to be angry about. But angry she was. It was an important emotion, one that got her into being an advocate for children, one that made that advocacy credible to the kids she works for, and the one that has kept her at it.

Q. What got you started? What got you going in this direction? Obviously this comes out of a lot of anger at something.

A. You bet it does. Back in 1964, I got a phone call from a friend. I had been involved in children's services, but on a very ladylike basis, serving on boards and committees and so forth, and I was President of our Jewish child care institution here in San Francisco and Vice-Chairman of the Jackie Committee, which is our foster home finding committee, at that time. I got a call from a friend of ours who knew I was interested in children's services. He said, "I don't know what this is all about, Jean, but a girl that's working for me"—he was director of the Actor's Workshop here—"as a set designer is on the phone on another line. She's in hysterics. They've got her baby up at the Juvenile Hall and they won't give him to her. And she says they've got him in a cage."

I had toured that place any number of times, with the United Crusade, et cetera, et cetera, and I had organized orientation tours for Jackie Committee members and I'd never seen babies in cages. So he says, "Is there anything you can do?" It was about seven o'clock at night. I said, "Where is she?" He said, "She was thrown out of the Hall, she's in a phone booth up near Juvenile Hall." I told him to tell her to wait up there and I would make a phone call and see what I could do.

Q. How old was her baby?

A. Just three years old. He had wandered away from nursery school. He hadn't been missed because the nursery school thought that he was with the mother and the mother thought he was at school. He had been in line, waiting for the nurse—it was a public nursery under the school department—and he had wandered away. She had two children there. The older one stayed and the little one just wandered away.

He'd been picked up by the police, taken to City and County Hospital after waiting at the police station to see if a call would come in for a lost baby and it didn't. So they took him to City and County where they examined him and found that there was nothing wrong with him except he was scared to death and wanted his mommy. So then they called the police back and they took him out to Juvenile Hall, and he'd been there all day.

When the mother went to pick the two kids up at five-thirty or six o'clock, there was only one child and she was panicked. The principal and the parents got all excited and they finally traced the child—first to the police station, then to City and County Hospital, and finally to Juvenile Hall, where they wouldn't release the baby till morning when a probation officer could "investigate the matter." The principal was there with them when they went to Juvenile Hall and he said, "It's not their fault. No one was negligent. It was an unfortunate incident. Give them their baby." But they said no, they couldn't have their baby till ten o'clock in the morning, when they could talk to a probation officer.

But they insisted on seeing their baby and they were taken back—after they were given a lot of static about it, they were finally taken back. They had these "isolation cubicles" and they routinely isolate everybody for forty-eight hours upon admission so they shouldn't give a germ to somebody else. And there was their baby in this isolation cubicle, bare walls, bare floor and an iron crib with a hard net tied over it to make a cage out of it.

Well, when the father saw the baby and the baby saw the father, he tried to get out of the cage and the father got excited and tried to rip off the net. They called some attendants and they threw the parents and the principal out of the place, and told them not to come back until ten o'clock in the morning.

I tried to phone the Hall. I knew none of this at this point except that they had a baby in a cage, and no one answered the telephone at Juvenile Hall. I tried to get Tom Strykula, whom I knew—the Chief Probation Officer. His phone was unlisted. So we called the judge. My husband's an attorney, so we knew a lot of the judges and we happened to know Judge Cronin. I've met him on, you know, civic committees and so forth, and I talked with him. I told him about the appeal that was made to me, I didn't know what it was all about, but something must be wrong. You can't insist on keeping babies in cages and not giving them to their parents. And he laughed and said, "Well, these things happen, you know. If you'll go up and vouch for the parents, I'll order the child released. I'll phone out there."

So we went over to the Hall, it's only five minutes from here, and my husband went out to find the parents at some gas station at a telephone booth, and I went in to talk to the Night Superintendent. I said, "This doesn't make sense. I don't understand it." He said, "Mrs. Jacobs, I don't make the rules. If we get a kid on a delinquency charge and parents show up who seem like responsible people we have rules where we can release 'em. But if a kid's lost we have no rules where we can release 'em."

So my husband came back with the parents and the principal and I insisted on seeing the baby where he was. He wanted to send an attendant to get the baby and I said no, "I want to see him right now." He gave me a lot of static and I offered to phone the judge again and get permission and he didn't want me to phone the judge again, so he took us back there. And sure enough, here was this isolation cubicle with this infant, this baby in a cage.

But this time, the baby didn't cry, he didn't try to get to his parents, he was like an animal with palsy. He just stood on all fours, shaking like a leaf, his eyes as big as saucers. He was completely traumatized, like he was catatonic. And when they took the net off and picked the baby up and handed him to his mother, he didn't even hold her. He just was like an animal. He didn't respond to her at all. They had failed him once and this time he didn't know what to expect and I'm sure this would leave a mark on the child for life.

Anyway, the parents said thank you and they left with the baby and I've never seen or heard from them since, but I came home and I couldn't sleep. And I raved and ranted to my husband about it until finally he said, "For god's sake, let *me* sleep."

Well, first thing the next day, I phoned Tom Strykula, and I told him that I wanted to see him. He said, "I know what this is about. This is about that—baby. Look, the baby's home with its parents, everything's all right." I said, "You're out of your mind that everything's all right if this is the way you treat children." I said, "I want to see you." He said he was very busy, had lots of appointments, so I said, "Tom, you will either see me this morning or I will be up there with a newspaper reporter, with photographers and I'll blast this all over the front pages of the newspapers." Then he said, "Come right over."

So I went over and I was so indignant and told him how I felt and he said, "Look, we have psychologists, we have psychiatrists, we have social workers, we have probation officers, we have all kinds of professional people who know what we do, who have established these procedures and who, obviously, approve them." He said, "What am I going to do? Tell them Jean Jacobs doesn't like it? Who's Jean Jacobs?" So I said, "If your doctors and psychiatrists approve this kind of care, then *they* should be put in cages." He said, "Would you like to tell them that?" and I said, "I certainly would."

So he took me down to see the doctor who was on duty. It turned out to be a woman who was an absolute animal. I wouldn't trust my dog, whom I love, to her. Turned out later, she got her kicks from giving little girls vaginal examinations. Anyway, I told her what I thought of this. And she says, "Mrs. Jacobs, what medical school did you graduate from? What are your credentials?" I said, "You don't need degrees to be a human being, and it isn't human to treat children in such a fashion." So she said, "There's no point in discussing this with you, Mrs. Jacobs, you're obviously very emotional about it. You don't understand what the problems are. You know, with what happens to these children before they come to us, it really doesn't matter what *we* do to them afterward. We can't harm them anymore.

And that was the beginning.

Q. How did Strykula respond to all that? Did he get nervous that you heard what you heard?

A. No, he was rather apologetic and took the attitude that I didn't know what their problems were, that really nobody cared or these kids wouldn't be there in the first place, that they do the best they can with what they have, that everything's a matter of budget.

Q. A game that Eric Berne should have put in his book is "you have to understand my position."

A. Exactly. So I left there and I was just bound and determined. . . . At that point I didn't know anything about delinquents, and I had no concern about them. I was concerned about this "cottage" full, there were thirty of them at the time, of *babies* under five years old.

Q. Under *five?*

A. Under five. Thirty babies under five in that cottage. The infants, the ones that aren't yet walking, are kept behind a glass wall and these abominable doctors who were more concerned about a germ than they were about the traumatic effect of the emotional deprivation that they were responsible for, wouldn't let a volunteer or even staff except for doctors and nurses touch those babies.

Q. Up till what age?

A. Up till one. And some of them were there for months and the only time they got picked up was to have their diapers changed or be fed. They were turning these babies into vegetables.

Q. There have been some pretty clear studies of that.

A. Of course there have. You change the emotional development of *monkeys* by this kind of treatment. Can you imagine what you do to human beings?

Q. Just to jump ahead in time a bit, does that facility still exist?

A. Oh, yes. It still exists. And then we have two others that are cottages for older dependent children. These are kids who have not committed a sin or a crime in their lives. These are kids who have been sinned against or whose parents can't cope or who came home one day and their parents weren't home. They have a cottage for older girls and a cottage for older boys. In the older ones they have little kids from five years old to eighteen.

Q. Is there any program for them?

A. There is nothing. The School Department is supposed to run a school program there.

Q. What do they spend most of their days doing? Watching TV?

A. No, they're locked in their rooms. They can only watch TV during the so-called recreation period, for half an hour or an hour.

Q. These are *dependent* children that you're talking about, not delinquent kids?

A. Yes. When they're in their rooms they're locked in. When they're out of their rooms, they're locked out.

Q. Now we're still talking about dependent kids now. How many hours a day are they locked in their rooms?

A. Most of the day and all night.

Q. You call them cottages. Are they cottages?

A. No, they're cell blocks, not cottages. And as for your asking about these being dependent kids, there is no difference in the way kids are treated except they comply with the law by having a separation, a physical separation. But the staff is interchangeable, policies are the same, everything is the same for the kids who are abandoned and the kids who are there for other reasons.

Q. When did you decide to get an organization together?

A. I formed Citizens for Juvenile Justice at the end of

JUVENILE HALL DISCIPLINE REPORT

In the event you confine a child to his room, or impose some other form of discipline that extends beyond the time your shift ends, you will complete this form in triplicate. Be specific and factual. One copy remains in the cottage and two copies are forwarded, via the Night Book, to the Superintendent's Office. This is to be completed prior to the end of your shift. Do not use envelopes.

CHILD'S NAME: *Martha X*   COTTAGE: *C-2*
AGE: *14*   DATE: *5-11-66*
P. O.: *Richard Meaglis*   DIVISION: *Family Intake*

OFFENSE: *Chewing gum*

DISCIPLINE: *24 hours—standard discipline for this offense*

J.H. #114

Kathleen Poston
—————————————————
COUNSELOR'S SIGNATURE

This is a discipline report from a "C" Cottage, a cottage for dependent children—kids who have committed no crime or offense but have been abandoned or taken "for their own protection" by the court. The punishment noted on the report as "standard discipline" is a twenty-four-hour lockup, allowing the child out of confinement only to go to the toilet. The girl was in Youth Guidance Center because the court felt her mother was mistreating her.

1966, after attempting to work through established channels and established organizations and getting absolutely nowhere. So we formed Citizens for Juvenile Justice and the first thing we did was to ask the Juvenile Justice Commission to hear us and to hear our complaints. In California, in each county, by law there is established a Juvenile Justice Commission which is charged, by law, with overseeing the administration of juvenile justice within that county. It is supposed to be the citizens' watchdog of the juvenile justice area. But it is also part of the state law that Juvenile Justice Commissioners shall be appointed by the judge of the Juvenile Court.

Q. That's like the fox guarding the hen house.

A. Exactly. So the judge appoints people who agree with his point of view or who are his political pals or his drinking buddies.

Now we have a law in California known as the Brown Act, which is the secret meeting act. It provides that all boards and commissions must hold public meetings with notices of meetings posted and regular dates and times scheduled. However, our judge used his Juvenile Justice Commission as a private little lunch club and they met in a little lunch room up on the third floor of Juvenile Hall. And they would not open their meetings to the public.

So we made noises about the Brown Act, and demanded that they open their meeting and hear us. So in January, 1967, they held their first open meeting.

We told them that we had organized Citizens for Juvenile Justice, what it was all about, who the members were—CJJ has a most respected and respectable group of professionals on the Board—and we offered to cooperate with them and to assist them in interpreting what the needs of children are in the community and to help them to get better services for the children. We wanted to be very cooperative.

After we finished our presentation, telling them what we thought some of the grievances were, some of the things that were going on that we frowned upon, the President of the Juvenile Justice Commission turned to the judge who was sitting right next to him and he said, "Would you care to respond?" The judge did care to respond.

He responded that "Mrs. Jacobs is a totally irresponsible person who does not represent the community"; that "all of these people are unofficial"; that nobody had appointed them; that "these were irresponsible charges"; and that "the only purpose that Mrs. Jacobs has in bringing these charges is to remove me from my position and get my job."

Q. Are you an attorney?

A. No—the whole thing was preposterous.

Q. Well, that would make it openly preposterous.

A. Right. But it was obviously a battle then, and unfortunately the press loves confrontations and personality squabbles and they saw this as being just that. If you look through the press clippings you'll see that everything comes out as being Mrs. Jacobs against Judge O'Conner and Judge O'Conner against Mrs. Jacobs. That kind of thing. They just all at once tried to bury our demands for institutional change under some petty personality clash. It was a perfect way to lessen our credibility, and it wasn't even a tactic. The press just likes a good fight between two people they can count on to put on a good show. It almost doesn't matter what your position is. You just become entertainment. But we stuck with it and didn't just go away and hide. We came back week after week and year after year, and they started listening to what we had to say.

I spoke to Jean again in February, 1972, two years after our first meeting and asked her about progress. It was hard to disagree with the goals of Citizens for Juvenile Justice, but I knew that getting there was another thing. I started with the babies.

Q. What happened to the babies in cages in Juvenile Hall?

A. Well, most of them are now being farmed out to what used to be a shelter for unwed mothers, but we still have babies in cages and we still have dependent children there.

Q. Weren't there commitments to change that?

A. Oh, yes, definitely, but commitments mean very little unless those who make them mean them.

Q. What about progress on other fronts for CJJ? How has it gone?

A. We managed to convince our Board of Supervisors to appoint a Delinquency Prevention Commission and I was appointed a member of it, along with some political appointments and some others who were really interested. One of the things that we were able to do was to look for Federal funds for alternative programs and get a group of consultants, people from various universities and from various kinds of professional backgrounds, to work with us. We got funding for a Chinatown Youth Service Center. That was the first. Now we have been able to get funds for four other Youth Service Centers. These were alternatives for kids to try to keep them out of Youth Guidance Center.

A group of these centers are now joined together to get licensing for foster homes and placements—developing programs for dependent children in their indigenous neighborhood. Two of the Youth Centers are in black ghettos, one is in our barrio, the Mission District, one is in Chinatown and one is in a lower middle-class white section.

The five of them have now gotten together to work through the process of developing a program and getting licensing so that dependent children can be cared for by their own people in their neighborhoods. This takes it out of the hands of the courts and welfare and bypasses the established system. As usual, when you're starting something new, there are all kinds of difficulties, but I think eventually it'll happen.

Q. What did you have to go through personally to move the CJJ from a no-clout position to functioning with some kind of power?

A. Well it was a political battle. I was able, knowing people in government, knowing some legislators, knowing a lot of university people and so forth, to get a lot of people moving. I personally had nothing to gain or lose so I couldn't be attacked. My job couldn't be taken away from me and I knew people. So we were able, for instance, to get our local Assemblyman to introduce a bill in the State Legislature (this was one of the earliest things that really had any significance) mandating that the Youth Authority establish standards for Juvenile Hall. There were none.

Q. Were you satisfied with the standards?

A. No, no. But a least they were far better than what existed, and at least it gave the Youth Authority a mandate to examine Juvenile Halls yearly to see whether these minimal standards were adhered to. Prior to that they had no authority even to go in and look at them.

Q. Then you really feel that the amount of time you've spent has shown some definite results?

A. There's no question that it has, because now people are conscious of the fact—at least in San Francisco, and in some other communities as a result of the publicity in San Francisco —that something is wrong with children's institutions and that something can be done about it.

Q. What would you say to people around the country who may want to get involved in juvenile justice and for whom there is no local group existing for them to hook into? Can they do what you did?

A. I think they can, provided they get a small nucleus of people who will take an honest look at what is happening and get as sick to their stomachs as we got, as I got, and as angry as I did and aren't willing to put up with that feeling. They have to be willing to put up with the discouraging, long battles that it takes to take one step forward. Usually it was very easy to rally hundreds of people around what they thought was a crisis situation because they had just been exposed to it. But once the flags and publicity around it go, the glamour of fighting a crusade is dropped by the media. Then the real battle starts because then it becomes day-to-day needling of those who are responsible and watching of those who are responsible. Unless you constantly watch, things revert back to the *status quo.*

Q. Why do they revert back? What is it that you're really up against?

A. Well, most of the force is bureaucratic inertia.

Q. So it isn't that they hate kids, it's just that they aren't as concerned about them as they are about their jobs.

A. Exactly. The minute you start criticizing a bureaucratic system of this kind, and you have as we have here a system which is completely autocratic and run by one judge, when you criticize that system, you are criticizing the judge and this makes people nervous.

Q. You had goals a few years ago that included more child-serving agencies, neighborhood facilities for kids, changes in Youth Guidance Center or Juvenile Hall, and you've achieved an enormous amount. What are your present goals and what's coming up?

A. Well the battle now is to close our two reform schools— not Juvenile Hall, but the reform school, which is the step before they go to the Youth Authority, which is the step before they go to our state prisons. We're in the middle of a battle now, having two hearings before the Board of Supervisors, and it's under submission. We're attacking them on three grounds. First, because they are enormously expensive and completely ineffective. Second, because the youngsters committed there are primarily black and minority kids and the institutional racism that is going on there must be stopped as it is clearly illegal; and third, because we have now established community centers, youth service agencies, and organizations that are willing to develop their own programs. They must be given the political and financial power that must be relinquished by the established agencies in order to let them succeed.

Q. Where do you see the CJJ going? What will your priorities be, say, for the next few years?

A. Once we get past these local battles and close these institutions, we plan—we've already started, as a matter of fact—to get legislation changing the laws which make certain acts crimes for minors that would not be crimes for adults. We want to get these off the books and we'll automatically cut the crime rate in half.

Q. Because things like truancy and "wayward minor" wouldn't be crimes?

A. Right.

Q. If you had to go back and start over or if you could go back to that phone call in 1964, would you do it again? Would you do the same thing, would you do it differently, or would you do it at all?

A. I would do it. I would do it a little differently, but not a great deal. I've learned in these years that I've been working in this thing that it's all very well to try to get a lot of professional people involved, but I have found that their involvement is short term. If I've learned one thing, I've learned that children and children's problems are very low on everyone's priorities. I mean those in high positions, those in positions of bureaucratic authority or political authority.

Q. Do you have any idea about why?

A. Well, I think primarily because those that are involved are poor, black, Puerto Rican, and minority-group people who are not a great concern to those in high places. It's part of the racism of this country.

Q. Doesn't the fact that white middle-class kids are getting arrested more for drugs and for political activity or whatever —hasn't that changed the nature of the institutions?

A. No, no. Too many of the parents of those white middle-class people want to write those kids off. They're turning their own kids in and this is one of the big problems.

Q. Doesn't it get in the way of positive institutional change when the society seems to want to grind these kids up?

A. It definitely does, but my great hope is the fact that the eighteen-year-olds have now gotten the vote. I have great hope and great concern for our young people today. They are humanistic and they are concerned with human values.

Q. Most of the things we're talking about, like juvenile institutions, came about as replacements for really bad systems and quickly became bad themselves. Margaret Mead called them "good ideas gone sour." How do we deal with that kind of human corruptibility so that five or ten years from now somebody doesn't have to start an organization to investigate those neighborhood centers that we both advocate? Do we have to have some kind of constant watchdog?

A. I think there has to be a constant watchdog but again I go back to the young generation growing up that feels that human values are more important than bureaucratic security. This is my hope.

Q. The place that I think maybe you and I would part is that I think what you say about young people is rhetorically true, but when it comes to implementing the day-to-day work that it takes to make any system human, I don't think kids are any better than their parents.

A. Well, I'm more optimistic than you about that. I've seen

and talked with and watched in operation an awful lot of young people who are so beautiful and so aware and so sensitive to human problems and human suffering that I'm optimistic enough to believe there's going to be a new direction. And if there isn't—God help us all.

5

Kid Jail Carousel: A Capella

Plans are almost complete for the addition of a juvenile detention quarters in the basement of the Ohio County [Kentucky] Jail. Judge Andy Funk and Jailer Floyd Albin took members of fiscal court on a short tour of the proposed facility Monday morning and explained the needs for having a place to separate young offenders from older inmates. . . . Judge Funk . . . said the basement detention quarters will accommodate six juveniles and will help keep the youngsters from feeling they are being contained in jail.

Ohio County *Times*, June, 1971

Proposals to allow ninety-day jail sentences for juvenile offenders and to eliminate the right to a jury trial for a juvenile committing a misdemeanor will be recommended to the 1972 Colorado Legislature, a committee of lawmakers decided Wednesday afternoon.

Denver *Post*, October, 1971

More than one thousand juveniles in Texas Youth Council institutions claim that courts committed them without legal representation in violation of state law and a U.S. Supreme Court ruling.

Houston *Chronicle*, January, 1972

James Archambault, administrator of the [Kentucky Juvenile Defender Program] . . . explained that the whole idea for the . . . program came from a noted Supreme Court decision involving Gerald Gault, a fifteen-year-old Arizonan. The youth was charged with making lewd telephone calls and, after an informal hearing, he was sentenced to a reformatory for six years—until he was twenty-one. Had Gerald been an adult, the maximum sentence would have been two months in jail.

Chattanooga *Times*, January, 1972

The girl was just thirteen years old and was in the county jail of a nearby community. She had committed no crime, nor had any charges been placed against her.

"They told us she had been hanging around with an eighteen-year-old boy and they put her in jail to keep her from getting pregnant," according to the lawyer who arranged her release.

Chattanooga *Times*, January, 1972

Nine long years ago, Dorothy had a quarrel with her parents and landed in the Diagnostic and Detention Center. As a result of that vivid experience:

She cannot drive into the neighborhood of the center without becoming extremely frightened, feels that she may be "warped," and may be doing damage to her own two daughters, tends to assume that persons who represent authority are likely to be malicious. Her marriage is threatened by sexual problems that she traces directly to her experience at the center, and she cannot stay in a closed place—an elevator, or a doctor's waiting room—without being frightened.

Louisville *Courier-Journal*, November, 1971

The Hampden County [Massachusetts] Training School in Agawam spent $8 more for veterinarian services in 1971 than for fees to doctors and dentists, a check of records indicated yesterday. It also spent $48 more on haircuts than on all medical services, including bills from doctors, dentists, and hospitals. Only seven boys at the school apparently visited a doctor during the year and only eight went to a dentist.

Boston *Globe*, February, 1972

The escape of three fifteen-year-old boys yesterday afternoon from Youth House, 1221 Spofford Avenue, Bronx, swelled to sixty-one the total who have fled the institution in the last eighteen months, THE NEWS learned yesterday. The number of breaks has been the subject of an inquiry by Commissioner of Investigation Louis I. Kaplan. He was spurred on by complaints of guards and counselors about the "permissive" policy of the detention house authorities.

New York *Daily News*, July, 1959

The chief medical officer of the Illinois Industrial School for Boys in Sheridan has testified that he frequently gives powerful tranquilizing shots to troublesome inmates. Dr. Victor Smith admitted he administered the tranquilizer, Thorazine, to asthmatics without examination. The drug can be harmful and sometimes fatal to asthmatics.

Chicago *Daily News*, June, 1971

Six persons—one of them a state probation officer—were indicted Wednesday in the Dade Grand Jury's continuing investigation into alleged drug abuse, illicit sex, and beatings at the county's youth detention facilities. The indictments bring to eight the number of persons charged. . . . Charges against them are, for the most part, contributing to the delinquency of minors. . . .

Miami *Herald*, October, 1971

A disabling chemical spray is being used at the State Training School for Boys [at Boonville, Missouri] to quell student disorders. Walter DeClue, superintendent of the school, said the chemical had been used about a dozen times in the last few months because "we have no alternative."

Saint Louis *Post-Dispatch*, January, 1972

A sixteen-year-old Brown Avenue youth was found hanged at the Juvenile Detention Home about eight A.M. Thursday morning by a University of Tennessee student who works at the home, police said. . . . Knox County Medical Examiner Dr. Ira Pierce ruled the death suicide. Authorities said [the youth] had been convicted Wednesday in Juvenile Court on charges of breaking into Lawson's Restaurant and taking $75 in cash and twenty cartons of cigarettes.

Knoxville *Journal*, July, 1971

In a blistering letter on conditions at the Youth House for Girls, Manida Street near Spofford Avenue, Bronx, the Grand Jurors Association of Bronx County yesterday charged that animals in the zoo have better housing than the child inmates of the institution.

New York *Daily News*, May, 1960

Following a visit to El Paso County Juvenile Detention Home late Thursday afternoon, District Judge Henry Pena, judge of the new Domestic Relations Court of El Paso County, described conditions at the home as "deplorable" and the home itself as a "shameful stain" on the community. . . . He added that he has been to the zoo at Washington Park on many occasions, "and animals and birds have better living conditions. . . ."

El Paso *Times*, June, 1971

The Virginia Juvenile Vocational Institute in Russell County, designed to handle only the toughest of the state's juvenile delinquents, is having disappointing results in its work rehabilitation program. Of eighty-five boys released from the institute since it was set up in 1967, one-third got into trouble again and another quarter is now unemployed.

Norfolk *Ledger-Star*, April, 1971

Warning that the riot in the Bronx Youth House is "only the beginning of an explosive situation in the City's detention homes," Assemblyman Max M. Turshen (D.-Brooklyn) said today he will sponsor legislation to "create more and better youth homes."

New York *Post*, March, 1957

Maryland's archaic and crowded juvenile jails boiled over last weekend with seven escapes, a homosexual gang rape and beating of a fourteen-year-old Montgomery County boy by other inmates, and ended with one jail converted into a segregated all-black detention center.

Washington, D.C., *News*, November, 1971

Pine Hills School for Boys has had five, six, or a dozen suicide attempts in the past year. The number depends on which counselor is questioned. Most of the boys tried to slash their wrists with sharp stones or glass. Two tried to hang themselves and one almost succeeded before he was discovered. . . . Boys can be sent to Pine Hills for offenses ranging in seriousness from an incorrigible runaway to a burglar.

Billings, Montana, *Gazette*, July, 1971

6

Preliminary Plans for Alternative Families

You have had a look at some of the problems of kids and their prisons. Now comes the hard part. What does it all mean? What, if anything, can be done to make bad situations better? What should we work toward?

Understanding must come first. If we rush blindly into battle with children's institutions and their keepers without understanding how and why they happened in the first place, we would be letting ourselves and, more important, tomorrow's children in for more of the same. I have a few ideas about how and why. I hope you add your own insights to mine and share yours with me. Understanding our own inhumanities, while only one step toward change, is nonetheless important. The danger is that we stop there. I will offer some suggestions for action for those who feel, as I do, that they are no longer able to give away their proxies for the care and education of our children to people who have proven only their ability to destroy and to deceive.

The fact that the public does not know about actual conditions in children's prisons (or about their existence, for that matter) is, on the surface, the main reason for their perpetuation. The "reform schools," "training schools" and "detention centers" are kept out of the way of the public in every possible way, beginning with their geographic location. Most of them are in the most inaccessible parts of states or cities, parts that average people don't pass through. Their inaccessibility keeps them away from the public consciousness—and the public conscience.

Little is written about these prisons for children except when the press finds scandal, usually after a child has been killed or after a riot or other massive violence.

Americans are victims of a perceptual illness, which might best be called the facial tissue syndrome, characterized by a selective and chronic oblivion to anything "distasteful," beginning with one's own waste matter and continuing on to the waste matter of society. Once we have called something "waste" it is cloaked in euphemisms and closeted out of sight. We have all become conscious of the word "ecology," which, after all, is nothing more or less than man's relationship to the place he lives and the delicate balances that exist there. Unfortunately, people make a distinction between the new consciousness about what our obliviousness has done to the air and the water and what such disregard has meant to the people we live with. Such a distinction, such self-deception, will prove even more deadly than our indifference to where we put our tin cans, our paper, and our smoke.

Anyone working for social change must assume that the public is ignorant of the problems he perceives. He must work first to erase that ignorance. But the fact that the public is *chronically* uninformed is symptomatic of its unwillingness to be informed, to see the unpleasant side, and, more basically, to assume the responsibility to act that an awareness of unpleasant information might demand. That, more than any other single factor, is what keeps children and others living in uninhabitable institutions. Spiritual laziness. Letting people pull the wool over their eyes because they don't really want to see. "Protective reaction strikes," wiping our behinds with "facial tissue," "training schools," and "guidance centers."

We are deceiving ourselves, and prison wardens and children's jailers feed off that self-deception. They didn't create the atmosphere. Children's prisons are hidden from our sight, not just because the institution has something to hide, but because we have asked that the institution be hidden. When the inevitable disasters happen, when children die or are so badly damaged that the public must be told, we can protect ourselves from responsibility by being "uninformed." We hire committees and commissions to figure out new ways to keep us uninvolved. The public is almost always informed about the things it really cares about. Kids, regrettably, aren't very high on the list.

Robert Ardery, in *African Genesis*, tells us that it is not man's innate aggressiveness that is so much a problem as his unwillingness to accept that condition and deal with it. As long as our basic tendency toward aggression is ignored, Ardery argues, instances of it, killings and wars, will be seen as exceptions and not as the rule. So it is with our children and how we keep them. If we can examine some of the reasons why we *hate* them as much as we do, maybe then we'll be able to love them. If we stopped playing dumb, our kids might grow up thinking that we're not so stupid.

Having informed an uninformed public about the state of their kept children, having discussed that elaborate denial mechanism we call adulthood, we can move on to more structural problems—problems whose solution awaits only the concern and involvement of the once uninformed.

Within the system that keeps our kids there is a conspiracy to prevent any humanizing change. There are three *status quo* conspirators: the civil service, the unions, and the professionals. Born out of struggle and exploitation themselves, civil service and unions offered great hope and progress at one time or another to the poor and powerless. Civil service came in as a reform move to counter the politicians' control of jobs under the spoils system. Unions develop out of the exploitation of the worker by big industry and had a hand in the cessation of destructive practices of child labor. Professional groups offered the public some kind of accrediting body that would assure them higher standards of professional care and treatment. All important reforms. But for the institutions that now affect children, these reforms have, as far as children are concerned, gone full circle, and represent the legal and organizational base on which the exploitation of children now depends.

Where civil service offered an equal opportunity for a job on the public payroll, it now blocks opportunities to upgrade publicly supported jobs and to demand better quality, higher productivity, or increased performance. It has become next to impossible for progressive programs to be instituted in existing juvenile institutions because most civil service commissions demand that workers be fired only for misconduct and only after lengthy administrative procedures. On the surface this might appear "fair" and "just," but in practice it prevents change from taking hold. Upgrading programs demands upgrading of people. Just because an administrator can't prove that a youth institution worker raped or beat a kid doesn't mean that the worker is caring for the child or developing the kind of relationships necessary for the child to care for himself. The absence of felony does not qualify someone to work with lost and troubled kids. Neither does seniority. Just as institutional changes, like the ones you have read about here, depend on new people and ideas coming in to replace old and worn-out ones *at the top*, the same factors hold throughout the organizational chart. Good people need good people to work with and while some existing staff can be "upgraded" by effective in-service training programs, it must be possible, when it is necessary, to kick out the bad staff and replace it with good. I am not suggesting the end of civil service, but an updating and upgrading of its standards and ideals. New evaluation techniques must be used to determine the effectiveness of anyone working with children. People failing to meet minimum standards must be removed, possibly transferred to less sensitive jobs in other agencies or divisions of government. The fact that a person can qualify to carry mail does not make him qualified to care for our kids. In most states the civil service standards for mail carriers are much higher. Check in your own city or state and see if you agree with the standards for child care workers. If you don't—get them changed.

Patrick Murphy, the Police Commissioner of New York City, has said many times that the civil service regulations were a major obstacle in upgrading the police. "When civil service is taken to the extreme so that somebody says 'you can't make me work,' then it has gone too far," Murphy said. I would add to that, that when civil service workers are offered more protection than the people they are working for, there is, at least, a need for equal protection under the law. Most of the terrible incidents in the institutions you've just read about would not have happened if the workers involved were convinced that such equal protection existed, and that their jobs depended on their proven competence.

Hand in hand with the low standards of the civil service is the unions' readiness to strike if the standards, low as they are, threaten anyone's job. In most institutions where new leadership has attempted to innovate, unions have resisted new demands on their workers. In many cases strikes and slowdowns have undermined reforms and caused legislators to regress to programs and practices that were proven failures. In one case, one of the most destructive institutions ever housing children was kept open after five government studies found it unfit because the union threatened a citywide strike. The issue was job security for its workers. No one was concerned for the security of the children.

Unions emerged because people were being treated as less than human. Ironic that they would stand for children being treated inhumanely, and that the justification for such a stand would be money. Talk to the head of your local children's institution. You will find that there are other ways that the selfish interests of institutional workers have taken precedence over the welfare of the children. It is not coincidence that in this country two of the most oppressed groups of people are the young and the very old. Neither has a union or an effective bargaining agent. Maybe the time has come.

Professionals are the third of the *status quo* conspirators. This is the elite corps of people who have been told for so long that they have the holy secrets, that they now believe themselves holy. It should be obvious that the medical and psychiatric teams that are either permanent staff to children's prisons or employed on a part-time consultation basis, have the greatest responsibilities to the children and the community to make certain that these institutions are fit places to live. These are people with the least to lose, the most "job security," and the greatest capacity to be heard by the public and the legislatures. Yet it is a most rare exception when any of them speaks out. Standards of medical and psychiatric care for the children in youth institutions are abysmally low in all but a handful of the nation's youth institutions. Medical and psychiatric associations should be formally notified of the conditions under which their members are practicing and of the low standards of care that their members are providing. Then, if they don't add their weight to pressures for change, class action damage suits and malpractice suits should be instituted against their members. Public hearings should be held to investigate the professional standards of these associations.

But standards, as they apply to the professionals' role in maintaining poor quality in childrens' institutions, can be a source of great hypocrisy. Where their own standards are low, professionals apply exacting and lofty standards to others, to "non-professionals" or "para-professionals." In fact, for everyone but themselves, the professionals in children's institutions are the standard *setters* and *enforcers*. Good people with good ideas and great capacities—like Jean Jacobs of San Francisco—are challenged by institutional professionals on the basis of their lack of credentials, while the professionals persist, with credentials, in support of destructive programs. Any citizen who attacks institutional practices is open for criticism, regardless of the validity of the attack, simply because "the professionals know what they're doing." They don't. If they did, the institutions that imprison children either wouldn't exist or, at least, wouldn't be in the terrible condition they are in. On one hand professionals know all the answers and everyone else should bow out. On the other, they should not be held responsible.

Professional people, like anyone else, will assume as much power as they are allowed. The assumption of corresponding responsibility is another matter. That is up to an informed public and the public's willingness to call a fraud a fraud and a failure a failure, even if the people responsible served time in universities. Somewhere, on our journey toward public responsibility for our children, all of us must renew our native ability to detect the truth and the sham. We must awaken our ability to act on what we see and feel. To trust ourselves.

Social workers are another story. We don't need them at all. A fake profession, social work exists only to convince people that the hell they are living in is really not so bad, and to collect large salaries for their trouble. Changes in institutional structure imply, at least, changes in their function. Social workers, sealed into their non-profession after years of monopolizing the institutional administration of child care, have the most to lose by the development of non-institutional alternatives. The elitist attitudes of the social worker, attitudes that are expressed as superiority and condescension toward parents and the public, have no place in the future.

We need a new discipline—call it a profession if you must —a new specialty of training that combines appropriate segments of psychology, education, medicine, nutrition, law, and other fields into a major discipline in child care that would prepare young people for careers as Child Advocates. These C.A.s would be specialists in children, their care, education, development, and protection. They would be our society's answer to the growing number of homeless kids. Professional parents.

Minimum salary for a C.A. should be set at the median income for physicians. They will be on the same kind of twenty-four-hour call that we expect from doctors. They will give up privacy and an eight-hour day for their commitment to kids, their problems, and their survival. Certification of C.A.s should be allowed only after two years of successful work with children, sufficient academic preparation in or out of school, and co-sponsorship of another C.A., three parents, and six people under eighteen. Right now there is no meaningful preparation or certification for people to work with our children. Isn't it about time?

After understanding comes action. What good going through the pains the children endure, seeing the potential that individual action has to stop or to lessen that pain, maybe even understanding some of the reasons that society and you have let children suffer so long, if, after all of that, nothing happens? There are ways for you to change the direction of institutional care for children—enough ways to fit into your particular style, needs and limits.

First thing is to get the facts yourself, first-hand. Don't accept the handouts or the words of the public-relations people. Tear up your proxies. You might get your own group together and visit, especially at night or on weekends, the children's jail nearest to you. Look it over and see if it's good enough for the kids that live with you, or other kids you know and care for. Talk to the people who work with the kids. Let your gut tell you what kind of people they are. Do you trust them? Spot conditions that might be improved and offer your talents or resources or suggestions to improve them. If the place needs books or records and you have some, give the lot to them and get your friends to do the same. If you're in the clothing business get the kids clothes if they need them. Do what you can do; do what you know. Use your imagination; the kids need it all. If it's just visiting every now and then, fine. It's important that these isolated institutions be visited. That, by itself, creates a safer environment. People are less willing to inflict their craziness on kids if they think someone might be looking or might find out. The history of injury to kids in these jails has persisted in isolation.

Many places just won't let you in. They'll use a broad range of excuses. The most common is "rules and regulations." "We can't let just anyone in here, you know," and "we must, of course, protect the children." Ask to see the rules and regulations. If they really prohibit all visits, which is unlikely, call the newspapers and your legislators and get them to visit the institution with you and to change the rules. If a "no outside visitors" rule does exist, you can bet the institution is among the worst. In general, you will have to get approval to visit, and this is understandable. But approval should be made on general standards and not on the whim of a public official who may have a lot to hide. Most places won't tell you that you can't visit. They'll just try to run you around so badly that you'll disappear. Many institutions told me that they were undergoing construction or being painted and I should call back in a few months. I told them that I was interested in coming anyway, and I did. Whatever the initial response, and it will include a good deal of surprise, the main thing to remember is to persist. If you really want to get in, you'll find a way.

Once you've made it in, get others to do the same. The important thing is that you begin and that you let yourself get involved in what appeals to you. Pick a place that suits you and stick with it; be consistent in what you do and what you give.

While any and all public involvement will change and upgrade the quality of care, one particular kind stands out. Pick out a kid and follow him along. Just be his or her friend, the person who will make sure that no harm will come. I'm not talking about a formal relationship like foster parentage or adoption, but about a relationship between an adult and a kid, based on the needs of both to survive. Kids need you to care about them while other people are caring for them. Adults need increasingly to be needed, validated. Pick out a kid in one of these institutions, get his name and talk to him, write to him, see him when he gets out. Let a lonely and frightened girl have someone to go to for help. Find out a kid's birthday and send something. Get your group to adopt this as a project. Civic groups and women's organizations, to mention two possibilities, could do much to offer locked-away kids some hope.

If you're legislation-minded, and have the time or the contacts, work to influence the legislature in your state to close existing large institutions and to establish human standards for all children's facilities. Support attempts to innovate by removing legal or administrative blocks.

Some people can offer kids a place to live. Foster-care placement is simple in most cities, and the rewards can be great. Most cities offer reasonable amounts of money to support such care and pay for medical, dental, and clothing costs. Kids that get a ready-made family to live in have a much greater chance. An extra seven- or ten- or sixteen-year-old in your home will undoubtedly change your life some and offer some problems. But if you can do it, you're offering someone a unique chance at life. Not too many people have the opportunity to give life to someone. Caring for an abandoned kid, however temporary that care needs to be, offers that opportunity. Keeping a kid out of an institution most often means keeping him alive.

If you are not yet certain that you want to initiate anything like I've suggested, don't go away. There are many people around who could use your *support* in what they are doing. These are people inside and outside the juvenile justice system who are working for change—and succeeding. Their continued success will depend on the numbers and support of people who will add their names and energies.

In the northeastern part of the country there are some pitched battles currently in progress. Jerry Miller, the Commissioner of Youth Services of the State of Massachusetts, has begun to close the large destructive kid prisons in that state. From the time he came into the picture a few years ago, he has worked for institutional reform. The employees, their unions and associations, and the legislators who blindly listen to them attempted to undercut each one of Miller's many attempts at reform. Workers threatened walkouts. Regulations were used to the letter to embarrass Miller, to force him out. Finding reform in his state impossible, Miller reacted with the sensibility of one who has come to understand institutional logic. He recommended that the institutions be phased out. Massachusetts had nothing to be proud of in its history of caring for children in trouble. Now it may. The small homelike alternatives that Miller is advocating will have troubles of their own, but in the end may hold the answer for the future.

The Governor of Massachusetts, Francis W. Sargent, took Miller's recommendations seriously and has announced plans to abolish the use of county training schools as penal institutions. He has also put forth a legislative program which would repeal all laws that treat truancy and habitual school absenteeism as crimes, and the "wayward minor" and runaway as a criminal. Instead, Sargent proposed that a civil court could rule such kids "children in need of supervision" and could recommend four courses of action:

1) permit the child to remain at home subject to supervision by a court clinic or a social service agency;
2) remove the child from home temporarily and transfer legal custody of him to a relative or a private child care agency;
3) transfer custody to the Department of Public Welfare for care in foster homes, group homes, or specialized treatment centers;
4) refer the child to the Department of Youth Services, which would pay for the care of the child in a group home, treatment center or foster home.

Sargent believes that this major change in the treatment of the children of his State would save dollars—more than one million dollars a year—as well as kids. And as if this wasn't enough to make him stand out as a major political Child Advocate, he also gets an award for having told a legislature eager to study youth problems that "they have been studied enough." Governor Sargent and Commissioner Miller are in for opposition and will need all the support they can get. Let them know they have yours.

Sargent and Miller have been fortunate to have the support of a journalist—Tom Marinelli of the Springfield *Union*—who *should* win a Pulitzer Prize. He has kept the issue of children's prisons before the Massachusetts public with remarkable passion and clarity, and has presented a body of information that any well-intentioned citizen could hardly ignore. It would be nice if other journalists would follow Marinelli's lead—nice but unlikely. See what you can do with your local press.

Jean Jacobs and the Citizens for Juvenile Justice in San Francisco are trying to get California to commit itself to a plan like Miller's and Sargent's. If you're in the Bay Area, you can help influence the State Juvenile Justice Commission to follow Massachusetts' lead.

In Louisiana, Luke Fontana has been working for a number of years to improve the conditions in institutions like Scotland-ville. A lawyer, Luke has gotten very deeply involved with kid jails in the most important way a lawyer can get involved: getting kids out and forcing changes that save kids still in. Since children's jails in Louisiana spend between twenty and thirty times less per year than, say, New York or Massachusetts, they also have the biggest built-in excuse for ignoring the problem. People like Luke Fontana, who force states to meet the requirements of their own laws and who provide kids some kind of constitutional guarantees, are forcing legislative awareness and action directly affecting and improving the amount of money and concern available. Lawyers are essential for forcing change, and more young lawyers like Luke need to give some time to developing plans and strategies to get kids out of these prisons. There are far too few interested in fighting battles for kids who can't pay and who rarely even say thank you.

Goodrich Walton is about to retire as head of Youth Services in Colorado. He will leave just when the institutions he has worked with for so long are changing direction in a way that makes his years of concern clearly worthwhile. But the boys' school at Golden is still trouble, and the girls' school will have to be watched in Walton's absence. Colorado people have a chance now, because of people like Walton, Mylton Kennedy, the former Director of Youth Services, and Ted Rubin, the juvenile court judge, to have a model system. Their own proven experiment in Boulder, where volunteers have replaced institutionalization, have proven them capable. It all depends on whether enough people there can get together to give the extra and sustained push that major change demands. Get to Ted Rubin at the University of Denver Law Center and find out what you can do.

Nationally, the Institute for Juvenile Justice is working to establish independent citizens' groups in every city. If you are interested in helping form such a group in your area or are interested in being part of a local juvenile justice group already existing, let them know. They are at 540 East 13th Street, New York City 10009.

The Institute is involved in many grass-roots battles. It goes into communities where kids are in immediate danger due to institutional practices and where the people have not been able to work out solutions alone. Able to fight the battle in the courts or from the streets, the Institute is the only group I know whose staff includes young people who know the realities of institutional life as well as people skilled in juvenile law, community organization, media, and alternative systems. It maintains a small staff of trouble-shooters ready to assist anyone working to better the institutions and services that affect children. The Institute is in constant need of money; since, as might be expected, it receives no support from government. Individual and foundation contributions are essential.

My own hope is for "new families," groups of people who come together for the support and security once found in "natural" or nuclear families. I think such groups could well care for most dislocated kids. They should come in many sizes, shapes, and styles, and appeal to different personalities, interests, experiences, and geographies. What they would have in common, these families-by-affinity, would be a capacity to provide basic relationships to people old and young who find themselves alone.

I believe these new families can reverse the pattern of disaffection and alienation caused or fostered by the breakdown in the nuclear family. People's needs have not changed as much as their surrounding institutions. Perhaps they have increased. The need for identification and familial support is not limited to the young or imprisoned.

From the commune or free school to the increasing number of professionals who are dropping out from established career patterns and dropping into "humanistic alternatives," the signals are clear that many people are looking for themselves in groups of other people. The question is whether we want to pick up that signal and see the way inhumanity and isolation affects the kids we are concerned with here.

People getting together in affinity groups called families could, initially, "adopt" kids within an institution, visit them regularly, provide for their needs, and watch out for their welfare. If the family or any part of it began to live together, kids could move in, too. Support could be arranged either from resources in the family or from "foster care" or other arrangements with local child-care officials.

I look to these new families for an answer because I think the time has passed when we can isolate or compartmentalize our most basic problems. Kids who are alone and isolated need least of all to be put with other isolated kids in a separate part of the world. They need most of all to become an integral part of something that has to do with old people and young, black and white, and all parts of living. I believe this is true of many of our existing "treatment" institutions, but especially true of our prisons. The more we foster difference, the more we should expect it. We need to reintegrate people, not disintegrate them.

I haven't the answers for all the possible questions and pit-falls that will be imagined and suggested about new families. But the facts are clear: students, businessmen, "street people," professionals, are looking for some sense of community; their isolation and the isolation of the institutionalized child are both destructive; many people are unhappy with existing answers; the resources exist to support new families. Put the pieces together your own way if you want.

Nor am I suggesting that affinity families are "the" answer. Some kids and adults need more specialized care—some need to be isolated. But for the bulk of us, young or old, new families, however we personally define them, hold promise.

We know there are people working, groups moving, and a system in some places edging toward change. There are jobs large and small for people who want more broad and decisive change. But there are one hundred thousand children still in bondage and we must be careful not to let small victories obscure or diminish the horrors children now suffer behind institutional walls. We have seen before in history instances where slight reforms and apparent progress have led to more severe repression. If we don't act with conviction now, that is what will happen. The progress of the past few years will be negated and kids will be worse off than ever. The forces to make that happen are waiting in the wings.

As with any change in any system, the key to understanding its direction is to understand the existing balance of power. In the kid prison system, that balance seems to be shifting slightly toward the kids. But on the other side stand our children's keepers, with clear vested interests and an uncanny knowledge of the people who give them power. They know us well—our ambivalences and our fears, our susceptibility to jargon and to ready answers, and most of all, our willingness to let other people handle our difficult problems.

Any long-range solution to the problem of our kept kids is going to have to start fresh—looking at who we are and what our problem is—and not be bound by past commitments or failures. We are going to have to begin a new relationship to our kids and to ourselves, a relationship that will have no place for keepers.

7

The Town on the Edge of the End

by Walt Kelly

The Town
on the
Edge of the End

Millions of years ago in the Land of Tomorrow and the Next Day there was a town, a tiny town, that might have been bonny and bright, but it was sorrowed and sore with a night that stretched through its days.

The night was a sadness and a black shadow made of many shades, a gloom cast by the presence of monsters.

They hung about in the trees and in the eaves. Some were goblins, short ones and fat, tall ones with a hungry look. Some were fiends with smoking hair and scaly hands, greedy lips and gritty smiles. There were smirking spiders and flat, round dragons, like pancakes, filling the fields. Great greasy toads sat in the doorways, trading maggots and swapping flies. The market was a snarl of snakes and nameless nidderings.

Food was snatched from the fork. Bed was impossible. The people of the town spent much time burning incense and muttering magic incantations, but the magic seemed to work badly. The plague of demons grew worse. Beating on pans did no good. An age old remedy for the horrors it was, but now no good.

Mighty speeches by men of government and stern proclamations by the Mayor against the slithering horde were listened to by the people.

These strong words caused the people to quake and children slumbering fitfully on their mothers' shoulders woke screaming and with the hiccups.

But not a round-eyed monster blinked.

Then one morning when the sun shone everywhere else, a fluting was heard along the ridge. Such goblins as had ears pricked them up and stopped chewing. The people of the town, tumbling over toads, rushed from their houses and looked to the hills.

Down the mountain road, picking his way between the flopping black things, there stepped a piper. His notes looped and soared and seemed to lift him over the gloom. The shadows seemed to part. Children with old tears still wet, laughed and clapped their hands.

Straight to the Mayor he strode. He flourished the pipe from his lips and bowed. *"Greetings, sir,"* he cried. *"You should be rid of these dragons."* The Mayor, combing lizards from his beard, replied, *"We know."* *"I shall take them away for you,"* declared the Piper.

A wombat leaped from beneath the Mayor's coat. The poor man shook a nest of salamanders out of his pocket and sighed. *"How?"*

"With my pipe."
"If you do," grunted the weary Mayor, *"You can name your own price."*

The Piper ejected a small beast that had burrowed into his pipe. He eyed the Mayor sternly. *My price is a promise.*

"Name it!" shouted the Mayor, stamping fiercely at a small band of scorpions.

"Once the town is bonny and gay...once it is fresh with air and clean with the sunlight...

then, you'll keep it that way." The Piper stood poised, his pipe before his lips.

"Done!" roared the Mayor. *"A ridiculous promise! Of course we will do it...We want it that way...."*

He tore off his trousers and pursued a small dinosaur that had been up his pant leg. *"Of course we'll do it."*

With that the Piper leaped in the air, cracked his heels together twice and a half, and blew a blinding note, the shrillest of shrill. Alighting, he set off at a crooked trot. He screeched broken notes and square notes, bouncing jagged notes and wriggling notes that twisted like eels. Wailing high as the wind, flatting low as a funeral drum, the pipe sobbed and screamed.

The people shut their eyes and stuffed their ears. This was worse than the monsters!

But then, the air around seemed to lighten. The children looked about them wide eyed. The goblins were leaving!

The sky was becoming blue!...The leaves of trees were lifted!
The grass stood straighter!...There was sunlight on the roadway!

The people gasped a mighty gasp...There, vanishing toward the rim of the world in the faraway west were the flying things, the scampering things, the crawling, slippery, scuttling things. They were following the Piper's manic tune. Soon they were gone and a bright peace was on the town.

Now the people of the town sat down to enjoy the sunshine of their doorways. They endlessly discussed the strange Piper. Some described him as tall like a thundercloud...some said no, he was more like a tree, a flaming tree. Others remembered that he was mounted on a plunging white stallion, and still others talked of the terrible sword he carried.

They were all agreed that he was magic, a supernatural magician. And what, asked the children, was the tune he played? That, muttered the elders with heavy head shaking, was a thing that defied description and which children would not understand anyway.

So the elders warned the children to be quiet and to be good. Walk just so, they said, and talk just so...and do not ask questions for which there are no answers because no one wants the plague to return. The old people sat in the doorways gossiping about the Piper and shushing the children. They haggled in the market place and wished the curse of the Piper upon those who traded with a sharper eye.

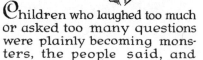

Children who laughed too much or asked too many questions were plainly becoming monsters, the people said, and such children were whipped soundly and sent to bed with the threat that the fiery Piper would come for them.

And all this made the elders very careful, and very solemn, for none of them wanted the return of the plague. They wanted the town to remain bonny and gay...They were quite determined to watch everyone very closely.

When, at last, the town had become a place of tiptoes and shushes and the people were fearful of moving quickly or thinking bad thoughts, it was noticed that the town seemed darker.

"It is the fault of the children," the solemn elders agreed, *"They are careless of the Piper's word. He warned us to be careful."* So all the children in town were spanked three times a day, before meals, and shaken well, into the bargain, on Sunday. Nobody wanted the children to grow into demons or monsters or even small fiends.

Then one day, when it had grown quite dark, a stranger wandered into town. He picked his way between the gossiping women in the market, he stepped over the slothful, suspicious folk in the doorways. He watched the sternfaced old men stamping away the children from their benches in the pale and seldom sunlight.

The stranger stepped up to the Mayor, who stood on the Town Hall steps. The Mayor was watching a child closely. The child looked as if it were about to laugh at a butterfly. The Mayor gripped his stick tightly and set his jaw. The stranger coughed.

"We should do away with those butterflies," rasped the Mayor. *"They cause trouble."*

"The town has the chill of night again," said the stranger. *"Have the monsters returned?"*

The Mayor looked at the stranger closely. *"We've done our best to keep them out. But, these children!"* He sighed and shook his head.

"Perhaps I can help you," suggested the stranger. He stepped into the street and from beneath his cloak he took a pipe. Setting it to his lips he blew three curling, dancing notes that seemed to lighten the sky. Children leaped and came running.

It was the Piper again. This time the music glided and sang, laughed and soared.

With lilting step the Piper danced off to the east, off toward the sunrise.

And this time the children, laughing with the notes of the pipe, followed, even as the demons had before them. Soon they were gone. *"He's done it again,"* murmured the old Mayor, *"for it was the Piper. He's saved us a second time."* The old man frowned at the butterfly. *"Be quiet,"* he cried, shaking his stick, *"Let that be a warning to you."*

If the butterfly heard, it gave no sign but fluttered raggedly off toward the lands that held the morning and left the edge of the world where night seemed to be settling, for good.